Nine Yana

Teaching on the Nine Vehicles according to the Buddhist Philosophy

AF755819

Khenpo Chimed Rinpoche

ADITYA PRAKASHAN,
NEW DELHI

First published in France in 2009 under the title
«9 jours pour 9 chemins - La voie du Dzogchen»
First English Edition, 2012

© Éditions Yogi Ling
La Galerie, 03 160 Ygrande (France)
www.yogi-ling.net

ISBN 978-81-7742-121-7

Rs. 450

Published by Aditya Prakashan, 2/18, Ansari Road,
New Delhi – 110 002.

email: contact@adityaprakashan.com
website: www.adityaprakashan.com

Printed at D.K. Fine Arts Press (Pvt.) Ltd., Delhi – 110 052.

Contents

Dedication

To my root lama, His Holiness Penor Rinpoche,
To His Holiness the Dalaï Lama,
To the high lamas of the Kagyü, Sakya, Gelug and Nyingma traditions,
To my sisters and brothers of France,
To all of them, my wishes of long and happy life,
May peace prevail in the heart of all sentient beings and all over the world!

and thanks

Linda Steven Pema Kunsang who wrote the French transcription,
Bruno Le Guevel who translated from Tibetan into French,
Myriam Zéghouani who translated from French into English,
Lama Sherab Namdreul, the publisher of Yogi Ling,
Fabrizio Frigerio Rigdzin Phurba,
All the Siddhartha Foundation family,
And all my brothers and sisters of France.

Khenpo Chimed Rinpoche

Foreword

Presenting the nine yana of the Nyingmapa Buddhist tradition, the ambition of Khenpo Chimed Rinpoche is to give the quintessence of the Buddha speech as well as the major commentaries of this speech during ages in the ancient India, Nepal, and Tibet. This book offers us also many amazing and edifying anecdotes about the life of the great masters and yogis that will delight the reader and nourish his daily thoughts. This teaching even approached basically, for the simple pleasure of discovery, will give incredible benefits.

This book is the transcription of a cycle of nine oral teachings given in Tibetan language, during the month of September 2008, in Strasbourg, France. Khenpo Rinpoche presented the 9 yana of the progressive spiritual journey that leads to Dzogchen, the pinacle of the spiritual realization. We have touched at the very heart of the highest level of Buddhist philosophy presented here in a very lively and accessible way and aimed at the public at large as well as for advanced practitioners.

We also hope that this book may help anyone who reads it: may it become a spiritual friend, a guide, and be a cause of Enlightenment for all beings!

May it be beneficial to all sentient beings!

Introduction

May the Great tradition of Khenpo Shantarakshita, Lobpön Padmasambhava and Dharma King Trisong Detsen increase and spread throughout the three realms of the World. May the appearance of the Three Jewels and the mindstream of beings remain inseparable, and bring sublime well-being throughout the three times.

The Tradition of the Nyingma School of Tibetan Buddhism

The Lineage of the Nyingma school of Tibetan Buddhist teaching is classified into three different types: The long transmission (Ring Gyu) of the extensive karma. The short transmission (Nye Gyu) of the profound terma. And the extremely short transmission of the pure Vision (Dag Nang) when teachings were directly received by the masters in pure vision from gurus and deities.

The Dzogchen Nyingthig Lineage of the Long transmission (Kama)

According to the Nine Yana of the Nyingma School of Tibetan Buddhism, the highest teaching is known as the Great Perfection (Dzogpa Chenpo or Atiyoga), which is the direct method for realizing the nature of mind and for attaining Buddhahood in this very body. Thus the Dzogchen Nyingthig, as a teaching, fundamentally deals with the expression of the doctrine of the Three Perfect Bodies (Kayas) of a Fully Awakened being, and this tradition has been transmitted through the three lineages of spiritual transmission as follows:

a) **The Wisdom mind lineage of the Buddha** This spiritual transmission is from the primordial Buddha Samantabhadra (Kuntuzangpo) of Dharmakaya to five self-manifesting Buddhas of the Sambogkaya. In this Lineage, the teacher transmits the teachings to the disciple, without using words or any other indications, only with his all pervading Wisdom mind.

b) **The Symbolic Lineage of the Awareness-Holders (Vidyadhara)**

The Sambogakaya Buddha Vajrasattva (Dorje Sempa) transmitted all empowerments and teachings to the Nirmanakaya Prahevajra (Garab Dorje), the first human master. It was from Prahevajra that this transmission was passed on to Manjushrimitra, Shri Simha, Jnanasura, Mahapandita Vimalamitra and Guru Padmasambhava (Guru Rinpoche). Here, an Awareness-Holder, a being who has direct and pure vision of the nature of reality, manifests to a receptive disciple and transmits the teachings by means of pronouncing a mantra or showing a sign.

c) **The Oral Lineage of the Realized beings**

Here the complete verbal empowerments and instructions are transmitted by words of mouth from the masters to the disciple. This lineage of spiritual transmission in Tibet initially spread through two traditions in the beginning at the early part of the ninth century. One tradition originated from Mahapandita Vimalamitra and is known as the "Vima Nyingthig". The other tradition originated from Guru Padmasambhava and is known as the "Khandro Nyingthig". Then, it was later that both these innermost Essence transmission met in Kunkhyen Longchen Rabjampa, from whom the uninterrupted oral transmission of these teachings have extended until the present day.

The Short Transmission of the Terma Tradition

The Terma Teachings are well known to have six lineages, since they possess three special Lineages over and above-mentioned Lineages. These are the Lineage empowered by enlightened aspirations, the lineage of prophetically declared spiritual succession, and the lineage of the dakinis' seal of entrustment. A more detailed description of these lineages can be found in Kyabje Dudjom Rinpoche's *The Fundamental and History of the Nyingma School of the Tibetan Buddhism* (With the English translation by Gyurme Dorjee and Matthew Kapstein and published by Wisdom Publication).

These Terma teachings were concealed mainly by Guru Rinpoche and his spiritual consort Yeshe Tsogyal, to be revealed at the time most appropriate for their discovery by prophesized "Treasure Revealers" (Tertöns), who are themselves incarnations of realized disciples of Guru Rinpoche. Guru Rinpoche first formulated the secret teachings by showing the method of attaining perfection (drub-t'ha) through the tantra, the method of attaining the core techniques (men-ngag) through perfection, and instruction on how to put these core techniques into practice (lag-len), with the blessings (mon-lam), the authority of initiation (wang-kur), credentials of authority (te-gya), future prophecy (lung-ten), and so on. Those secret teachings were then concealed in small boxes of terma. Furthermore Terma teachings (terchö) can be classified into three main types:

1) **Lama**

The peaceful and wrathful sadhanas on Guru Rinpoche, usually divided up into outer, inner, secret and innermost secret cycles;

2) **Dzogchen**

Teachings on Ati-yoga (DzogpaChenpo); and

3) **Thugje Chenpo (La Dzog Tuk Sum)**

Sadhanas of the great compassionate one, Avalokiteshvara.

These Dharma Treasures (Terchös) are the teachings which possess the "warm breath" of Guru Rinpoche himself. As there are no contaminations and errors in them, so they are extremely powerful, they have almost no obstructions for the practices, their accomplishments are easy to attain, and their fruits are swiftly achieved.

The Dzogchen Longchen Nyingthig Lineage of the Extremely Short Transmission of pure Visions (Dag Nang)

It was in the eighteenth century that the spiritual master **Rigzin Rangjung Dorjee Jigme Lingpa** (Who was the combined emanation of the Mahapandita Vimalamitra, King Tritsong Detsen and Gyelse Lharje, 1729-1798), received the complete Dzogchen Nyingthig teachings from Manjushrimitra, Humkara, Guru Rinpoche, Yeshe Tsogyal, Vimalamitra and Longchen Rabjampa, through the three lineages of Wisdom Mind, Symbolic and Oral transmissions, in the state of pure visions. In these visions, he saw Longchen Rabjampa three times and received his blessings of body, speech and mind. Thus, he became inseparable from the spiritual Master and attained the realization of the Great Perfection. These Dharma Treasures (Terchös), which were collected into nine volumes, became his own Mind Terma and came to be known as the renowned "Longchen Nyingthig" lineage. His disciples were scattered in all different schools of Tibetan Buddhism.

After his passing away, the "**Longchen Nyingthig**" lineage was propagated through his two main disciples: Jigmey Thinley Woser (the first Dodrupchen, 1745-1821) and Jigmey Gyalwai Nyugu (1765-1843). His incarnation included: Do Khyentse Yeshe Dorjee (1800-1866), as his body incarnation; Patrul Jigmey Chokyi Wangpo (1800-1887), as his speech incarnation; and Jamyang Khyentse Wangpo (1820-1892), as his mind incarnation. Nowadays the 'Dzogchen Nyingthig" and the "Longchen Nyingthig" are known as Earlier and Later Nyingthig traditions respectively.

The Buddha's teachings

Tashi Delek to everyone!

May you receive all my excellent and auspicious wishes and my best greetings. A special Tashi Delek to the translator. I am happy to see again those I've already met.

Among the people here today, there are some new persons and some more familiar. For the new ones, some of the points that will be dealt with hereafter may seem not clear enough, but I will do my best to make it as much clear and understandable as possible for everybody.

* * *

While listening to the word of Buddha, the Awakened Being, and while considering the different schools and traditions that have manifested to comment his speech, we can state that there have been many ways, some more subtle than others, to report it. The word of Buddha is not linear. Many interpretations are possible. Once you start to explore it, you discover how deep and meaningful it is.

Getting closer to the very essence of the Buddha's teachings, you can notice two main features: the deep aspect of the absolute reality (Skt. Dharmata, Tib. Tchönyi) and the vast aspect that deals with the five paths and ten bhumis (Skt. Bhumi, Tib. Sa), ten levels of realization into which the bodhisattvas and finally the noble bodhisattvas (Skt. Aryabodhisattva) are engaged. All these experiencing fields, the profound aspect of the absolute reality as well as the means to attain realization, are extremely large and not easy to master.

Trying to understand the Buddha's teachings, imagine that you start with this large field about paths and bhumis, you will first strive to get its meaning through explanations, syllogisms, scriptures commentaries, textual quotations and that will eventually lead you far away from any intellectual understanding, but instead to direct experiencing, to non-conceptual understanding.

As a matter of fact, you have to practice real listening and attention (Tib. Theupa) if you want to invest yourself in this very large field. You are the receptacle of a teaching given and explained by the master — it is actually much easier to study a subject while receiving oral explanations rather than only read them — but this must be followed by moments of reflection and meditation. This practice of attention is not like the western one — opening a book, skimming through it, intellectually understanding its topic then putting it aside and getting to the next one. According to the Tibetan tradition, we get involved in a process of closer and closer understanding of the teaching while thinking it over again and again. There is a first step just to get to know what it is all about on a quite general basis, and then we can have access to a more subtle level that will afterwards enable us to explore it deeper and deeper. This is the only way that allows us to really get a true understanding of the matter. This method is very different from the one used in the Western countries.

In Western countries, the word "Buddhism" is used in a very general way, but actually this term refers to the whole words and teachings of the Buddha, that is defined in Tibetan as "the spoken word of Buddha". We could almost say «the living word of Buddha, the Enlightened One, given over fifty years of teachings». After half a century of teachings, Buddha passed away into Paranirvana, into "Great Peace". Then all his disciples, who had followed him or had been attached to his philosophy, all these great masters of ancient India started writing and commenting his words as well as elaborating treatises to clarify his teachings.

In the West, the term "Buddhism" seems to cover an ideological whole including all the sermons of Sakyamuni Buddha and all treatises by great Indian masters explaining them.

In the Buddhist process, it is rather a practice to attain Enlightenment, a path made up of many experiences that will lead you to Buddhahood. This way differs completely from a conceptual approach. At the beginning, this Aryabodhisattva who was to be fully awakened and later on called Buddha, the "Fully Awakened", kept silence during seven weeks. He thought that his realization was an ineffable experience that could not be depicted with words, and trying to convey it through concepts would not help understand neither its meaning nor its reality. Therefore Buddha decided not to say a single word during seven weeks. The following parts of his lifetime sound much more like an allegory. Indra, the supreme king of the gods, as well as Brahma and other invisible livings appeared to him, imploring him to turn the Dharma wheel, that is to say, to teach this path to Enlightenment. As their request was sincere, Buddha granted it. According to this tradition, masters and gurus still proceed the same way imitating Sakyamuni Buddha. Teachings can only be transmitted when they are really requested, when there is a true and sincere thirst and craving to learn.

As he accepted to teach, Buddha went first to a place where he met his five previous companions in asceticism. There started the transmission. Sakyamuni Buddha insisted on the fact that no one should accept his teachings as such if they have not first been seriously analyzed and closely examined. He advised his disciples to behave like a goldsmith who, when given a piece of gold, first burns it, hits it with a hammer and deeply examines it. The point is to prove the consistency of the matter, to check if it can match our own experience and has got the power to transform us. Buddha encouraged his audience to keep a critical mind, to check the accuracy of his sayings and to find out in which way they can nurture their own inner experience.

This new Buddha, who was going to teach during decades had non-self-interest at all, since his realization was far beyond any worldly matters. He emphasized that everyone should wonder if his teaching could benefit one-self, stressing that teaching was for him of non-self interest. He was not looking for any kind of gratitude, glory or richness. He had no need for all of that. But far more important for him was to see that people, who came to listen to him, succeeded in integrating his words — that are relying on direct experiencing of Boddhicitta — to help them to reach at least the first level of liberation (Skt. Moksha, Tib. Tharpa). As a result, their mind would no longer be reborn freedomless, or at worst fall into the inferior states, but at best would be able to attain full Enlightenment. Buddha's only aim at his teaching is to help people to innerly improve themselves so that they will be free from any suffering.

The Baghavan's first motivation was to solve the problem of suffering. The spiritual path is a means to get out of suffering as long as the law of cause and result is firstly well understood (Skt. Karma) in order to gradually realize the ultimate, the nature of mind. This approach requires much more than a strict philosophical reflection that is most of the time only intellectual.

Investigating and analyzing

The teaching of Sakyamuni Buddha is not an even path of practices as it takes into account the different kinds of people and their large diversity of abilities, skills and personalities. Some people with strong capacities and great intellectual sharpness will be able, at first, to analyze scriptures that require logic and few other reasoning skills. But many people have neither time nor abilities to explore the different sutras and other treatises written through time after Sakyamuni Buddha had passed into Paranirvana. If these persons wish to go forward on the paths and bhumis, there is one mean, called trust or devotion, but it has nothing to do with blind faith.

Thanks to this trust, the Buddha's teachings on absolute reality, nature of mind and non-self can find an echo within ourselves. We can appreciate them as trustworthy. We trust these words talking to us about absolute reality, inviting us to respect karma rules. We trust our mind, that tells us, for instance to refrain ourselves from doing such and such things and so to avoid the resulting consequences. Without deeply studying scriptures, we can feel connected to this message. This is another way that enables us to go forward, as many cases through centuries have demonstrated it.

Trust and devotion

This method is applied to the basic practices which consist, for instance, of deeply thinking about the cause pattern, but also concerns more advanced practices in the Vajrayana, during the generation stage of the practice (Tib. Kyerim), which means to experience one-self as the deity, or during the dissolution stage (Tib. Dzogrim) where we are more focused on the subtle body winds. Even without any great knowledge, but nevertheless with devotion, it is possible to keep inside, like precious jewels, all the few simple instructions available to us, to fully integrate them and make them ours. So it is possible to progress on the path. Buddha said that doubt is the worst enemy on this path. Someone with great trust and devotion and able to keep them alive, can let grow anything virtuous and positive inside, whereas someone deprived from this devotion will not be capable to develop what is called «white dharmas»: loving-kindness, respect towards other people, diligence and energy put into practice.

On this path towards inner awakening, there are two methods: firstly, through attention and reflection, secondly through practicing inner integration of the received instructions.

1. First method: attention and reflection

Attention (Tib. Theupa), within an oral tradition, mainly means listening to the master's words and their explanations. It is all about listening to what Buddha taught, discovering the different streams of his thinking. There is a distinction between sutras that are rather an exoteric presentation and tantras in Vajrayana that imply greater sharpness of thinking and practicing. Some gurus use specific treatises to better illustrate the teachings. Once this base is acquired, the master invites the disciple to practice the second step, reflection. Through practicing attention can awakened understanding (Skt. Prajna, Tib. Sherab) arise. It is neither really wisdom yet, nor mental intelligence, as it is commonly understood in the West, but a kind of enlightened knowledge or cleverness that enables us to start considering things much more clearly. What about this reflection? When we are examining these different explanations closer and trying to understand them more personally, innerly, there are many contradictions arising, bringing with them uncertainty. Either we try to solve these contradictions by ourselves, or we go to a master and ask for precisions. The practice to eliminate uncertainty is called "Drodok Chödpa" in Tibetan. The practice to achieve a certain level of conviction and consistency upon a topic is called "Tenlapapa". It is followed by an experience of absolute certainty.(Tib. Nge She).

2. Second method: practicing inner integration

In all Himalayan regions, even if people do not go to monastic schools, the thousand-year-old tradition prevailing there creates such a cultural background that people grow in an environment naturally turned towards practice; they receive oral transmission and many of them become excellent practitioners. They receive instructions to practice and attain concentration, inner insight and can quite easily put the teachings into practice. In the West, as the cultural and spiritual backgrounds are different, you may be willing to start straight ahead, but you can not skip the essential stages where you have to deeply think about the teachings, check their consistency and make sure you have understood them clearly. But once this kind of foundation is stable, then you can develop your practice.

Eighty-four thousand stanzas, nine vehicles

The teachings of Sakyamuni Buddha are subdivided into twelve branches, building a whole set containing eighty-four thousand stanzas, displayed like quatrains. It is voluminous and inexhaustible. As an example, we can say that the Buddha's teachings look a little bit like an elastic we can stretch very long and far, but making it short, in its heart essence, it is all about our own mind.

While exploring this teaching, there is a non-ordinary way to proceed: not using the mental to understand, but instead opening up to these words. What comes next may be disconcerting for some of you.

On this path, it is primordial to develop trust, renouncement and universal love. Receiving teachings does not happen with an ordinary mind, we should open up our heart, listen from the very bottom of our inner self, so often deeply hidden within ourselves. This is the reason why there are three great distinct vehicles (Skt. Yana, Tib. Theg-pa), three great spiritual paths, three great yana. (Tib. Lam).

1. Hinayana, the first vehicle: Renouncement

Hinayana, the basic vehicle that enables the mind to mature, is characterized by the renouncement to the world, by not being systematically involved in it, but instead taking some distance from it.

Renouncement is the foundation of Hinayana. While being at the threshold of the path, if we do not aspire to renouncement or feel a sense of distaste for Samsara, at least a kind of weariness towards our own confusion, our uncontrolled mind and suffering that prevent us from experiencing blissfulness, obtaining the cessation of our sufferings in the bardo of becoming (Tib. Sipa). If we do not control our own mind, then, at the moment of our death, our consciousness will be propelled again into another birth through the power of our karma. Continuously arises the becoming with its sufferings, the Samsara. If we do not feel somehow sick about Samsara, then this kind of spur, that drives us to put an end to suffering, will be missing. This weariness helps us not to be prisoners of the becoming wheel anymore.

2. Mahayana, the second vehicle: Bodhicitta, Heart of Enlightenment

The characteristic feature of the second vehicle, Mahayana, the bodhisattva vehicle, is to develop Bodhicitta, which means opening up our heart, not focusing only on ourselves, nor being only seeking our own inner happiness, but to understand that the spiritual commitment interacts on a universal level and concerns all beings.

Bodhicitta, Heart of Enlightenment, is the foundation of Mahayana. If we consider our personal realization only, the main goal will never be attained. It will not be possible to reach this level of complete peace, of total elimination of suffering, called Nirvana. This experience of blissfulness can only occur when we are fully open to all sentient beings. Once we have been purified through different techniques and have "opened up our wisdom eye", then we will be able to realize this state of blissfulness. This demonstrates how relevant it is to develop Bodhicitta at this second stage and to manifest unconditional love for all beings.

3. Vajrayana, the third vehicle: pure vision

The characteristic feature of Vajrayana is to uphold the sacred commitments or samayas. Here we learn to develop a pure vision toward the deity and its mandala, the master and all beings.

Pure vision is the foundation of Vajrayana. Vajrayana is requiring even more than the two other vehicles. We have to develop a pure vision on all manifested phenomena and living creatures, on the whole world and all sentient beings. We have to see them as manifestations of deities. To attain this view of infinite purity, we have to hold the samayas, to steadily cultivate these sacred bonds towards the chosen deity practice (Tib. Yidam), as well as towards our lama, and all the beings in our environment.

In no way should we have upon them an impure vision. If we want to attain this view of infinite purity (Tib. Rabjam), we have to uphold our sacred commitments that are binding us to the yidam, the lama and the beings.

This path is demanding. It enables us to progress practicing attention, reflection and meditation. We have to go through several stages. For sure it is not a cerebral process at all.

The three pillars

The three pillars are renouncement, heart opening, (Skt. Bodhicitta) and upholding commitments that enable us to attain the view of infinite purity.

This introduction is a first approach to help us to set the scene and replace things and beings in their context. Following this path of inner Enlightenment is demanding: cultivating trust, renouncement, heart opening, pure vision, there is a lot to work on ...

Causal vehicle and fruition vehicle

While looking at the word of Buddha transmitted over fifty years of teachings, we can notice two great streams:

The causal vehicle of characteristic features includes Hinayana and Mahayana. In this vehicle we are still in mental representations. The characteristic features deal with this intellectual understanding of the path we have at this stage. We are not plunged into the heart of a direct experience.

Vajrayana is the fruition vehicle or vehicle of secret mantras. Its instructions are proportionate to the results we are longing for. When a consciousness is fully awakened, it looks at beings and places for practicing with a perfect pure vision, considering the former as deities and the latter as mandala palaces. Fruition is this view of infinite purity resulting from a fully awakened mind. It is called "fruition path" since its instructions match the final level of realization we wish to attain.

Why do we talk about causal path of characteristic features? Which result can we attain from that cause (Tib. Gyu) when it is cultivated? Here we are still in a dualistic view, the cause being different from the fruition or result. Many discussions may come from this point of view because there is a fundamental continuity, a link between seed and sprout. But seed is not sprout. To get a sprout, the seed must die. We are making effort to cultivate specific causes — at least to succeed in controlling our mind — like a seed we have sown. When all conditions and all favorable factors have been gathered, a change can gradually occur and hence, we can obtain some result.

In Vajrayana, the way to proceed is different. Instead of focusing on cause, we consider result reality or fruition reality. While contemplating this result in a direct manner, this reality is being actualized and thus will become a true reality for consciousness thanks to the path. "Being actualized" means to start being linked to this reality. From the vajrayana point of view, stating that everything is totally pure, that all beings can manifest as male or female deities, then, there is a means, right on the spot, with regard to this reality, to begin to feel connected to the reality of the deity practice, to our yidam. What was hidden is arising, unveiling and thus becoming reality. In Vajrayana, we do not think anymore that cause differs from fruition. This is like a shortcut: through concentration on fruition we are realizing it right on the spot. The only thing we have to do is to discover that this deity was already present within us, but we could not notice.

Sutrayana and Vajrayana

1. Three vehicles of Sutrayana

There are three vehicles referred to in the Sutras (Tib. Do). There is firstly Hinayana, including Shravakayana, the vehicle of hearers, secondly Mahayana and thirdly Pratyekabuddhayana, the vehicle of "solitary realizers".

2. Six vehicles of Vajrayana

Within Vajrayana, also called vehicle of tantras or vehicle of secret mantras, we must distinguish between the three sets of so-called outer tantras, comprising Kriya tantra, Charya tantra and Yoga tantra from the three other sets of so-called inner tantras, Maha yoga, Anu yoga and Ati yoga.

Summary table of the 9 yana

Hinayana and Mahayana, causal vehicle of characteristic features.

Three vehicles of sutra: rising vehicle through emanations.

1. **Shravakayana**, vehicle of hearers (Hinayana).
2. **PratyekaBuddhayana**, vehicle of "solitary realizers" (Hinayana).
3. **Mahayana**, vehicle of Bodhisattvas.

Vajrayana, fruition vehicle
The six vehicles of tantra are:

Three outer tantra: vehicle of knowledge through asceticism.

4. **Kriya tantra**
5. **Charya tantra**
6. **Yoga tantra**

Three inner tantra: vehicle of skillful transcending means.

7. Maha yoga

It deals with techniques of Kyerim, generating oneself in the pure nature of the deity.

8. Anu yoga

Once we are familiar with practicing pure vision, then we can work on channels and winds.

9. Ati yoga or Dzogchen, the Great Perfection, the peak of yoga practice.

Eight vehicles leading to the peak

We have drawn a brief table of the nine vehicles specific

to the Nyingmapa tradition.

But why do we talk about stages (Tib. Rimpa) ? The first eight vehicles are like steps on a ladder that lead the practitioner to the highest level, the supreme vehicle, the vehicle of Great Perfection or Dzogchen. These eight paths with their own methods and practices are, at this point of our inner development, like eight successive stages leading us to the last and highest step.

Three circles

This progression can also be figured out in three circles: firstly, the outer circle, secondly, the inner circle and thirdly the secret circle.

1. Outer circle

The first three vehicles, Shravakayana, Pratyekabuddhayana and Mahayana are building "the rising vehicle through emanations". It means that an awakened mind can infinitely emanate itself under multiple aspects and thus, help consciousnesses to rise. This is symbolized by the Samsara wheel, the becoming wheel, whereby a Buddha is pictured in each of the six realms. There are six guides. This shows that, in hells, as well as in the realms of hungry and thirsty ghosts, animals, human beings, semi-gods and gods, darkness certainly is everywhere, but active enlightening forces are also co-existing to guide beings and help them getting out of their state of confusion and suffering. The term "rising through emanations" means "every emanation an enlightened mind can produce to guide beings".

According to the terminology specific to the Nyingmapa lineage, these first three vehicles are called Kun Djoung Thekpa. Kun Djoung means origin with the underlying idea that a fully awakened mind, the mind of a Buddha, can infinitely manifest itself, under human or animal appearances or under many other invisible forms. In this context, "origin" refers to the extraordinary diversity of manifestations of an enlightened mind. These different emanations adapt themselves to the different beings, to the different realms. The many manifestations of a Buddha in the human realm take human forms. Kun Djoung means the extraordinary diversity of appearing forms an enlightened mind can manifest. In Tibetan, Thekpa means to drive, to guide. It means that every appearing form, that infinitely manifests, aims at guiding the confused consciousnesses and leading them to a state of realization, whereby they can recognize their true nature and awaken to their absolute reality.

The function of these vehicles of shravakas, pratyekabuddhas and Bodhisattvas is to pull practitioners out of this reality called «contaminated karmas and kleshas». They are used to enable beings get out of this truth of the origin of suffering, which is the mainspring of Samsara.

2. Inner circle

This circle comprises the three other outer tantra: Kriya tantra, Charya tantra and Yoga tantra, building "the vehicle of knowledge through asceticism".

This vehicle aims at acquiring the knowledge that involves the full realization of the absolute reality (Skt. Dharmata, Tib. Tcheunyi). At this point of his or her inner development, the disciple has not yet the ability to see that in the practice of Kyerim, "the samaya being" (Skt. Samayasattva, Tib. Damtsikpa) is actually making one with "the wisdom being" (Skt. Jnanasattva, Tib. Yeshepa).

At the beginning of the practice of Kyerim, also called practice of generation, we visualize ourselves as the deity with regard to the received empowerment. In a second step, we invite the wisdom being, the true nature of the deity, to merge in our heart, thus there is a kind of splitting between ourselves seen as the deity and the deity itself. In the three outer tantra, we are not able yet to experience this merging. We rather see ourselves like yidam's servants, or according to the Indian way, like yidam's worshippers. As sign of respect to the deity, we do our best to conform ourselves to it. As the deity is totally pure, we take great care of keeping strict body hygiene, by always wearing clean clothes after having a bath or a shower, by paying attention to the quality of food that has to be vegetarian, with regard to protecting life. All of this, of course, has to be understood in the Indian environment and context. The word asceticism is certainly too strong. More appropriate would it be to speak about a kind of discipline concerning hygiene of body, food and speech that should be respectful and smooth. This way of being and behaving enables us to attain realization and understanding of the absolute reality.

These three so-called outer tantra are defined as "vehicles of knowledge through asceticism" since a kind of discipline is required to be able to recognize the nature of mind. This path leads to knowledge.

3. Secret circle

This circle entails the three so-called inner tantra defined as "vehicle of skillful transcending means". In Tibetan, they say "Wangyour Thabpaï Thekpa". Wangyour means "attaining mastery over something", "becoming master of something". We gain mastery over something that was beyond our capacity, on which we had no control.

At the stage of Vajrayana, on the level of inner tantra, skillful means enable us to transcend the five poisons (Skt. Klesha, Tib. Nyeun Mong), the five conflicting emotions (ignorance, pride, jealousy, desire, aversion) into five wisdoms.

In the first three vehicles, "rising vehicles through emanations", conflicting emotions or torments as Buddha used to call them, are considered as poisons.

In the three following vehicles, "vehicles of knowledge through asceticism", conflicting emotions are rather regarded as something from which we should keep our distance. They are not perceived as poisons since we are beginning to understand how inherent they are to our mind, but still we try to keep them afar.

At last, on the third level, that of the so-called inner tantra, "the vehicle of transcending skillful means", that is to say Maha yoga, Anu yoga and Ati yoga, we can, thanks to the quality of our view, thanks to the power of mudras, concentration and mantras, transcend these five poisons, so that they can recover their true nature of the corresponding five wisdoms. This is the profound insight of Vajrayana realizing that originally there has been nothing but these five aspects of wisdom. Because of misunderstanding and confusions have these five wisdoms been gradually obscured and turned into five poisons. Nevertheless, thanks to Vajrayana, it is possible, at least through the methods of Kyerim, concentration, mudras and repeatedly reciting mantras, to go back to the very essence of the five poisons that are the five wisdoms. Therefore it deals with transcending.

On the level of the so-called inner tantra, the Vajrayana path is becoming very fast and very efficient. It does not require all the same efforts as needed in the previous vehicles. Unlike the three outer tantra, there are in Vajrayana no such requirements for strict body and food hygiene. When reaching the highest level or Dzogchen, continuously reciting mantras is not even necessary. It becomes a tremendously powerful and direct path that enables to fully realize the Absolute. That is why it is called the vehicle of skillful transcending means (Tib. Wangyour Thabpaï Thekpa) because it enables us to get freed from these poisons, and thus to control this energy and to transform it.

The Nine Yana

Hinayana

In the Hinayana, it is necessary to be inclined to renounce, to feel weariness towards the samsara (Tib. Khoroua), which means round or wheel. Why renouncement? We make the experience that there is no real essence in what we call the samsara. We become aware that living in the samsara means living in duality; being always driven either by likes or dislikes. This is the starting point of everything; this is how the samsara works. It is important to feel that the samsara is totally empty, that the samsara is just like a bad joke. In Tibetan, it is said that the samsara is like the hallucinations a complete drunk could have. When we begin to understand what this life entails, full of confusion, far from being the manifesting field of wisdom, but rather a life at the mercy of delusion, then at once we are seized by a feeling of sickness. Thus we are experiencing renouncement. This sense of renouncement should not be underestimated since it is the foundation, the ground, the common vehicle.

Mahayana

We then have to integrate the second vehicle, the Mahayana, the great vehicle of Bodhisattvas. At this stage we notice that the only longing for the extinction of sufferings, what is technically called Nirvana or moksha, that is to say Liberation, is certainly very praiseworthy, but there is still something even more immense to experience. When we receive teachings from masters about the aspiration and determination of Bodhisattvas, we realize that it is about our opening our eyes and we can see that every single sentient being is experiencing the same condition as we are. It is impossible not to be affected by this when it comes to practicing. Through our practice we should first train ourselves to avoid being unconcerned, secondly we should develop love and compassion which is naturally followed by an extraordinary feeling of deep personal conviction and a motivation to realize the Heart of Enlightenment (Skt. Bodhicitta) for the sake of all beings. Thanks to this energy of Bodhicitta, it will become possible to attain omniscience (Tib. Namkyen), a state whereby veils, even the subtlest ones covering our consciousness, are totally eliminated.

Through Hinayana, thanks to the feeling of renouncement and the application of different practices based on teachings such as developing concentration and sustained attention, it will become possible to attain Liberation, the cessation of suffering.

Through Mahayana, the energy of bodhicitta, which is at the very core of the practice by Bodhisattvas, it will be possible not only to experience this state where we experience the non-existence of suffering, poetically called Great Peace, but also to get our mind freed from any single veil and fully awakened to its true nature. Using this vehicle, we can undoubtedly come to know this state of full awakening, but it might take us a very long time, that is lifetimes and lifetimes.

Vajrayana

Through the third vehicle, Vajrayana, which is an accelerating vehicle, the progression is swift and easy. Why? True Vajrayana, not a carbon paper copy of Vajrayana, provides us with the means to get out of the dualistic view, to put a new perspective on reality, to develop a view of infinite purity with regard to ourselves, our body and thoughts, the whole world and other people. Vajrayana enables us to take another path. Instead of struggling here, looking at our dark parts and facing our demons, thanks to Vajrayana we can discover the luminous parts within ourselves, and hence progress more quickly.

Within Vajrayana, the fundamental power of Maha yoga is to generate skilful means; Anu yoga uses the energy of awakened awareness, which, once it has matured becomes wisdom; Dzogchen allows access to non-duality, to the perfect union of skilful means and awakened awareness.

Why does Vajrayana enable us to quickly and easily realize this primordially Awakened Mind? What is it that prevents us from being awakened to this primordial Awakening? Even if it is right here in front of us, why can't we see it? The transfer imprints of the three visions experienced at the time of death are indeed responsible for this non-recognition. When we are dying, three visions occur: a vision of infinite clarity, a reddish vision and a pitch dark vision. At that moment, we are drawn back again into the Bardo and hurled towards another birth. Why do these three visions — called "transfer visions" — arise? They appear because of karmic imprints (Tib. Bakchags), which are related to the energy received from our mother, the ovarian energy, and to the energy received from our father, which is called sperm energy in Tibetan. Furthermore, when the embryo is forming, according to the Buddhist point of view, a consciousness coming from the Bardo then joins the two other energies. This consciousness is a unique entity made up of a lung or wind and a mind. These three imprints, comprising the male and female gametes and the energy of the wind/mind, make these three visions arise when we are dying and therefore, once again, deprived of any freedom, we are hurled towards another birth.

Vajrayana enables us to purify these imprints so that our mind can be cleansed from all obscurations, even at the subtlest level, and we can fully awaken to its inherent nature of primordial Awakening.

This Nyingmapa presentation of the nine Yana, which are regarded as stages, helps us understand how we can gradually progress until we attain realization. Firstly, it is absolutely necessary, like hearers who want to become arhats, to have this sense of renouncement and aspiration for the cessation of suffering. But this should not satisfy us. For then arises the idea of skipping into the bodhisattva vehicle and with it the necessity to work on opening our heart, which is a crucial point of Bodhicitta. While this is a tremendous step forward, it does not allow to quickly realize Awakening. Consequently, we step into the next stage of the six-level presentation of Vajrayana. We gradually include the three outer tantras, followed by the three inner tantras, Maha, Anu and Ati yoga, which are extremely powerful, precisely because of their specific subtlety and because they can make the transfer imprints, left over from the three visions, completely disappear.

How can we integrate these different vehicles?

The word of Buddha with the Sutras, then the Shastras and the different treatises written by Indian masters, followed by those given by Tibetan masters obviously build up a tremendous amount of scriptures but, most importantly, they provide instructions for each of us suited to meet our individual needs. It is necessary to keep the essence of all these instructions, whose starting point is renouncement and whose end goal is attaining the vision of limitless purity (Tib. Dagpa Rabjam) specific to Vajrayana. Every instruction is like a personal message to each of us to guide us in our practice, quite a long message in fact as it consists of two hundreds volumes!

A genuine anecdote tells us that when the great Atisha went to central Tibet, he noticed that the people were far from being ignorant about buddhism. So he said: «There was actually no need for me to come here. You have the scriptures and you seem to understand them perfectly». But when Atisha started to question a few scholars of the time, he realized that the situation was not as good as it seemed on first sight. No doubt the scholars knew the different sermons of Buddha quite well and the various treatises that had been composed to clarify the word of Buddha. Then Atisha asked them the following question: «But when it comes to doing your practice, how do you proceed?» They answered: «First, we practise the different basic instructions of Hinayana which enable us to develop renouncement and all our practice is focused on this one point. Then, we concentrate ourselves on every precept of the Bodhisattva path, then, after a long and in-depth study of these different precepts, we move onto Vajrayana, to develop pure vision that involves seeing everything and the world itself as the deity palace». And Atisha exclaimed: « How stupid you are! Your understanding of the teachings is completely wrong! You have not attained the goal! ». So, what is that goal about? Then Atisha explained to them that they have to integrate everything into their practice, unify everything. The working ground should be weariness towards confusion called Samsara. From this basis, rather spontaneously and as a continuation of this conviction, they have to open up their heart and not only focus on the cessation of suffering, but, firstly and mainly, think about happiness and realization for all beings, for every single one. Then, turning to Vajrayana, they will be able to experience Awakening very promptly while deepening limitless purity.

The Buddha's teachings and instructions have to be integrated by each of us by keeping their innermost essence in mind so that we "catch the spirit of them". We have to be fully impregnated by the thought of renouncement. We have to stop our clinging attitude. Then, we have to develop our bodhisattva mind, a natural innate sense of nobleness, a sense of generosity from the deepest of our heart, we often did not even know we had, even though it is a true reality, and we need to allow it to express itself. Finally, we can climb to the next step towards pure vision by stopping our continuous tendency to judge, but still continue to be open-minded and open-hearted. In this way, the path becomes unique for each of us.

Hereafter is a somewhat simplified presentation of the nine Yana. The Buddha's teaching along these fifty years is not monolithic. It is dedicated to individuals endowed with specific sharp abilities (Tib. Rab), whose capacity to understand spreads far beyond any mental level. Then come disciples granted with intermediate capacities (Tib. Ding), whose capacity for sharp insight is lower. Finally, there are those people with more limited capacities (Tib. Tama). They need more explanations and their understanding is more mental. This presentation of the path in nine parts relies on the diversity of the disciples' abilities.

This classification can be even more detailed by showing the different intermediate levels corresponding to the different stages of uncovering our various veils.

Classification by understanding levels

1. Upper faculties with three subdivisions:

Superior upper faculties, medium upper faculties, inferior upper faculties.

2. Medium faculties with three subdivisions:

Superior medium faculties, medium medium faculties, inferior medium faculties.

3. Lower faculties with three subdivisions:

Superior lower faculties, medium lower faculties, inferior lower faculties.

It is a codified classification. Each level is associated with the corresponding thickness of defilements that can be discarded. According to a progressive presentation of the path, we begin with the thick-thick defilements, then the intermediate-thick ones, followed by the thin-thick veils. Then there are the thick-intermediate, the intermediate-intermediate and the thin-intermediate ones. Finally, there are the thick-thin, then the intermediate-thin and the thin-thin veils. All of them can be gradually eliminated.

Besides this classification in nine yana, we can sometimes find a presentation divided into one, two, three or five yana. Buddha said that if we take all different mental faculties of beings into account, we can estimate that there are as many yana as there are beings. But, at the same time, reducing it to the heart essence and trying to find out what an individual requires to spiritually open up and to attain full Enlightenment, we can suggest this progression on the path towards Enlightenment via these nine yana. It is also possible to synthesize the path into five or into two yana. In one of the nine great sutras of Mahayana, a teaching transmitted by each «historical» Buddha who has manifested in this world, it is said that there is actually only one single yana (Skt. Ekayana).

Four baskets and eighty-four thousand stanzas

Another classifying system of the Buddha's teachings provides a presentation in four baskets. Usually we mention three baskets (Skt. Tripitaka, Tib. Denö Sum) that consist of the Vinaya basket (Skt. Vinayapitaka), the Sutras basket (Skt. Sutrapitaka) and the basket of the upper knowledge of phenomena (Skt. Abhi-dharmapitaka). The fourth basket deals with the Vajrayana tantras.

The Vinayapitaka is a set of teachings related to the discipline that rules daily life and behaviour of monks and nuns and is generally applied in Buddhism whether it is in Hinayana, Mahayana or Vajrayana. Buddha pronounced these twelve thousand stanzas, (Skt. Sloka) to show practitioner how they can succeed in mastering their mind. Vinaya aims at attaining mastering of mind as well as upholding some specific vows. Even the upholding of only one vow can lead us to mastering our mind.

1. Vinayapitaka

The Vinaya basket comprises twenty-one thousand stanzas revealed as antidote against desire and attachment.

2. Sutrapitaka

The Sutras basket comprises twenty-one thousand stanzas revealed as antidote against aversion and anger.

3. Abhidharmapitaka

The Abhidharma basket comprises twenty-one thousand stanzas used as antidote against ignorance. (Tib. Timuk)

4. The basket of Tantras

The basket of tantras or Vajrayana contains twenty-one thousand stanzas that enable us to eradicate simultaneously the three following poisons: desire-attachment, aversion-anger and ignorance.

It is a set of four times twenty-one thousand stanzas, which makes a total of eighty-four thousand stanzas representing all the teachings of Sakyamuni Buddha.

The three poisons, either on the manifested level where they exist as seeds, as well as on a more profoundly hidden level where they exist as imprints, are the real problems we have to tackle. These three conflicting emotions must be eradicated in order to completely eliminate our defilements and allow our mind to fully awaken.

These three levels are considered as superior, intermediate and inferior practices carried out by individuals endowed with upper, medium or lower faculties. Individuals with lower faculties will then start with the inferior level of practice.

Three sacred pillars of Longtchenpa

The omniscient Longtchenpa mentioned "the three sacred points" that could be designated as three pillars or three preparatory stages.

1. First pillar

We should always develop Bodhicitta, the Heart of Enlightenment.

2. Second pillar

We should always be aware of being in a state without focal support.

Here support refers to our "mental". This means remaining in a dimension beyond the restricted mental framework.

3. Third pillar

We should always practice the dedication of merit.

This is underlined by the very words of Buddha who said that there are three main steps along a practitioner's path, which are as followed: "attention" which leads to "reflection" and reflection which leads to "meditation". During these three crucial stages on the spiritual path, whether we are at the "attention", "reflection" or "meditation" stages, we should be very careful that every one of our activities be permeated with this noble Heart of Enlightenment that blossoms through love and compassion towards the multitude of sentient beings. This positive attitude that is underlying within us will soon become a true determination to achieve Enlightenment to benefit all sentient beings.

When it comes to practice itself, we do not confine our practising endeavour on a mental level, or as it is said in the Tibetan tradition on the «mental mind support», but instead we are trying to remain in a dimension that overcomes the narrow framework of the intellect.

At the end of our practice, it is necessary to dedicate this view of the absolute that has been generated through the practice, so that, thanks to the power of wishes, it can become the cause of Enlightenment. Hence it would allow us to awaken ourselves to our true, primordially pure nature, and once awakened we might be able to perfectly serve all beings. This is the meaning of dedication.

Buddha declared that if we are always moved by these three principles that Longtchenpa will later call "the three excellent factors", then our practice will take on its true dimension. At first, if we care being in this state of inner nobleness and deep heart generosity, our practice will become fundamentally positive.

During meditation and when we listen to teachings, we should pay attention to be very open-minded, without judgement, like an immaculate page ready to be written on. This attitude constitutes the main part of the practice without any mental support. Then dedication comes at the end.

Having this quality of presence in the main part of the practice prevents this virtuous, positive energy from being destroyed by circumstantial factors. Within this quality of presence, whereby mental mind does not interfere, we can feel like being at the very heart of an indestructible reality. This a-temporal, non-created energy is really invincible. Through dedication, the positive energy will not decrease, but instead it will keep growing, evolving and enhancing.

It is very important — something that we are always reminded at the beginning of any teaching session — is to make the following three excellent factors our allies. I am going to mention them again to you:

1. In the preliminary stage of our practice session, the Heart of Enlightenment or at least have a noble, generous thought;

2. In the main part, the state without focal support;

3. At the end, the merit dedication allows merits to become the cause of our attaining Enlightenment for the sake of all beings.

4. We need to integrate within us the three great vehicles: the vehicles of the Shravakas, of the Bodhisattvas and of the Vidyadharas, also called Vajrayana.

Shravakayana, the path of the hearers

The hearer (Skt. Sravaka, Tib. Nyientö) is "the one who is listening". Shravakayana is the vehicle of the hearers since the practitioners on this path listen to all teachings, including the more advanced teachings, but they only put into practice a certain kind of instructions. So the hearers have been the receptacle of all the words of Buddha.

The mind of the hearer

A shravaka is moved by a deep and strong motivation to liberate himself from the samsara's sufferings to achieve this state of cessation of sufferings, called "Liberation". But his motivation is very self-oriented. Not that the shravaka is deprived from any compassion but his aim is limited to his own being. He thinks: « I can't do much for others, but at least I will do my best to master my mind and then I will be able to fully realize this reality that Buddha called the person's non-self. I am not endowed with this specific energy of a bodhisattva that enables him or her to work lifetimes after lifetimes on liberating all beings, but at least, I will work on my own liberation. Hence, there will be one being less in Samsara ».

Thereafter, through working on concentration and sustained attention, this practitioner puts all his efforts to allow his mind to properly focus and therefore totally penetrate that reality of the non-existing «I. This shravaka understands that this is precisely the concept of «I» that is responsible for the creation of conflicting emotions, passions

(Skt. Klesha, Tib. Nyeun Mong) and karma. He feels then a great aspiration to achieve the reality of the person's non-self.

Etymology

As we have just mentioned it, the sanskrit word "shravaka" (Tib. Nyientö) means "listening". The shravaka listens to everything. Even when Buddha taught the Prajnaparamita in Rajgir on the Vultur's Peak, shravakas were there. They were listening to the teachings on great emptiness. The shravaka's listening consisted of collecting the whole teachings. This was not a passive function since the shravakas used the collected teachings to propagate them to other people. In the Tibetan Canon (Tib. Kagyur) we can find the whole set of scriptures that contain the sermons and words of Buddha. In regard to the Prajnaparamita, sometimes Buddha was not teaching himself but it was one of his disciples Sariputra, Maudgalyayana, Ananda or Subuti. A sermon consists of exchanging questions and answers. It is very lively. Sometimes shravakas were asked questions, sometimes shravakas were questioning Buddha. Shravakas have played a major role in transmitting the living word of the Baghavan.

Shravakas are disciples of Buddha. Their function is to collect all the teachings and propagate them to others, even if they are not practising these teachings themselves. Shravakas are totally pure receptacles of the Buddha's teachings and therefore able to pass them on.

The six major linking points

1. What is the entrance's door? (Tib. Jugo) of the shravakas' path?
2. What is their view (Tib. Tava) upon things?
3. Which is their ethic?
4. How do they practise meditation (Tib. Gompa)?
5. What is their conduct (Tib. Chödpa) in their daily life?

6. Which results or fruition (Tib. Drebu) will they gain?

1. The entrance's door
2. The view
3. The ethic
4. The meditation
5. The conduct
6. The result

1. The entrance's door (Tib. Jugo)

The entrance's door is the four noble truths that we will develop later on.

2. The view (Tib. Tava)

The view consists of realizing the person's non-self.

3. The ethic (Tib. Tsültrim)

The ethic consists of upholding one of the eight sets of individual liberation vows, called pratimoksha vows. Some of them (five or eight vows) regard lay people, men and women, who commit themselves to uphold the five following vows: no killing, no lying, no stealing, no sexual misconduct, no taking of any intoxicating substances. Some other vows concern novice monks and nuns. Few others are meant for fully ordained monks (Pal. Bhiksu) with two hundreds and fifty-three vows and for fully ordained nuns (Pal. Bhiksuni) with three hundreds and sixty-four vows. The seventh set of vows entails the vows that a woman can take when she is between the state of being a novice and a fully ordained nun. The eighth set of vows involves vows taken while practicing for example Nyung-Ne whereby fastening is one of the vows.

4. The meditation (Tib. Gompa)

Firstly, it is about cultivating mental quiescence (Skt. Samatha, Tib. Shine), while practicing the nine stages of samatha to attain mental stability.

Secondly, it is about practicing profound insight or superior seeing (Skt. Vipasyana, Tib. Lhaktong). Once the mind is stabilized, a little bit like unclear water left to settle, it is possible to cultivate profound insight which consists of sixteen small truths resulting from a subdivision in four sets of each of the four noble truths.

5. The conduct (Tib. Chödpa)

The shravaka has to respect twelve learning qualities. It concerns life rules dealing with the right behaviour of the monk, still being currently in use in Southeast Asian countries like Thailand. For example, with regard to the way of begging mornings, holding the alms bowl in one's hand while looking downwards. The aim is to exert oneself to remain, whether on body, speech or mental level, in a state that is irradiating peace, which inspires lay people.

6. The result (Tib. Drebu)

The result, the fruition, is divided into four phases of which the fourth is ultimate, a point of no return. Practitioners engaged along the path of shravakas long for the cessation of sufferings or Nirvana. They wish to attain the state of Arhat. At this stage, whereby there is no reversing, the consciousness of these persons can no longer experience any samsaric rebirth. The consciousness is freed from the rebirths and deaths cycle.

Hereafter, we are going to examine each point in a more detailed way.

More details about the six linking points

1. The entrance's door (Tib. Jugo)

Regarding the four noble truths, some things have to be thrown away and some others have to be cultivated and developed. The four truths of these noble beings start with recognizing the truth of suffering. Hence, the shravakas investigate upon the truth of the cessation of suffering, and then they try to actualise it through the path, and lastly to understand its origin. Some things will have to be renounced, some others to be developed. Therefore, when compendiously summarizing it to its very essence, through this quadruple display, it is possible for someone following the path of the hearers to accomplish the full extinction of suffering.

It is also very often referred to the two following truths: the relative truth and the absolute truth. Within this perspective, these two truths are means to lead to properly recognizing what is happening on the relative level, namely the law of karma, and what is happening on the absolute level, namely the non-created dimension, otherwise called dharmata. The aim is precisely to determine both of these phenomena, from the relative as well as from the absolute viewpoint.

This four-level presentation, referring to the four noble truths, includes instructions which enable us to move along the path, first through recognizing our situation, which is a suffering state; secondly through putting into practice the corresponding instructions to get freed from suffering.

The three teachings about the Four Noble Truths

At Deer Park, located at about six kilometres from the present town of Sarnath, Buddha turned for the first time the dharma wheel, forty nine days after His Enlightenment, and made his sermon on the Four Noble Truths in front of his first five disciples, the very fortunate five, who were his former companions of asceticism. Buddha will give this teaching three more times in his lifetimes.

The first teaching on the Four Noble Truths

During his first teaching, Sakyamuni Buddha introduced the Four Noble Truths from the viewpoint of their reality: the truth of suffering, the truth of the origin of suffering, the truth of the cessation of suffering and the truth of the path leading to the cessation of suffering.

The second teaching on the Four Noble Truths

In his second teaching, the Baghavan expounded to his fortunate five disciples the Four Noble Truths from the perspective of activity and practice. How shall we stand with respect to each of these Four Noble Truths? To explain his teaching, the Baghavan replied with four sentences that every Buddhist practitioner should be acquainted with:

« The truth of suffering is something that must be recognized. The truth of the origin of suffering is something that must be abandoned. The truth of the cessation of suffering is something that must be realized. The truth of the path that is leading to realizing the cessation of suffering is a truth upon which our mind has to rely on». In Tibetan, the verb "tenpa" means "to trust, to rely on ". This means that this is an inner path in which we have full confidence, we can rely on it with great trust.

The third teaching on the Four Noble Truths

The Baghavan taught then his five fortunate disciples about the Four Noble Truths with regard to fruition.

Buddha explained that a boat is necessary to cross a river, but once we have reached out the shore, the boat becomes useless. When we have accomplished the final result, once we have gained the opposite riverbank, we become aware that there is nothing to be accomplished. This is relevant from the absolute perspective.

Once the other shore has been reached:

We become aware that there is no need recognizing this truth of suffering that requires to be recognized.

We become aware that there is no need abandoning this truth of the origin of suffering that requires to be abandoned.

We become aware that there is no need actualising this truth of the cessation of suffering that requires to be actualised.

We become aware that there is no path that would lead to the cessation of suffering and on which our mind could find any kind of support.

The entrance's door of the shravakayana path is the Four Great Noble Truths, each of them being subdivided into four truths that represent namely sixteen small truths. Facts are first expounded and secondly comes the cause. The truth of suffering is firstly explained and then we get back to the cause. The way to proceed is alike with the truth of the cessation of suffering and then entering the path that causes the cessation of suffering.

This deals with applying the law of karma. Something has to be abandoned, hereby the suffering, and something has to be gained, hereby the truth of the cessation of suffering.

The entrance's door into the Shravakas' vehicle consists of putting into practice the Four Noble Truths's instructions and meditating on them.

The Baghavan chose to deal first with fruition, the result of our ignorance, namely the truth of suffering. Actually, he intended to show that our body itself and its five aggregates (Skt. Skanda), shaped by our contaminated karmas on which we cling so strongly and to which we have identified ourselves, as well as the concept of "Mine", are fundamentally merely suffering.

The universe itself made up of the dynamics of the four elements in their impure dimension, is a cause of suffering. Everything is made out of the nature of suffering which can manifest in many completely different subtle ways.

Causality pattern (result/cause) to explain Samsara

The Baghavan expounded first the reality of suffering that is a result, an effect. To start with, a practitioner has to recognize suffering and then investigate on its origin or cause. «Where does it come from? Why does it occur »? From that questioning point we can get back to the cause. The cause is producing an effect. We have first to be fully aware of the result to be able to examine what cause has induced it. In Tibetan, "Kündjung" means the original location. Because of the five kleshas, composed of ignorance, pride, aversion, desire, jealousy and because of our contaminated karmas, all our activities whether concerning body, speech or mind, are distorted. Kleshas and contaminated karmas produce the origin of suffering. They have to be abandoned.

The cause and result principle shows how it is relevant in the functioning of Samsara as well as Nirvana. In regard to Samsara, the causality is the truth of suffering and the truth of the origin of suffering.

Causality pattern (result/cause) to explain Nirvana

Once we have understood what is the cause of suffering, it is appropriate to wonder if it has any ending. The Baghavan said that suffering can get to an end, that it can be totally eradicated. This is the reason why the effect is shown before the cause. When the practitioner is really evaluating the truth of the origin of suffering, he is wondering whether it can stop or not. It is quite logical to show first the truth of cessation and then the truth of the path leading to the cessation of suffering. Because, whenever we know that there is a possible end to suffering, then we seek for entering the path leading to that end.

Then come the fourth of the Four Noble Truths, called the noble octuple path that leads to the cessation of suffering. The eight aspects of this noble path are: proper understanding, proper thought, proper speech, proper action, proper means of living, proper effort, proper attention and proper meditation.

We can notice the relevance of these Four Noble Truths which are the entrance's door or starting point into the Shravakas'path.

Furthermore, we can see the intrinsic power of this presentation of the karma law to explain Samsara and Nirvana.

This general presentation has dealt with the four great truths of noble beings, but when we get closer and deeper, we can see that there are indeed sixteen small truths, since each of these four major truths comprises four subdivisions.

The four subdivisions of the Four Noble Truths

The first noble truth, the truth of suffering is divided into four aspects.

1. Impermanence
2. Suffering
3. Emptiness
4. Non-self

The second noble truth, the truth of the origin of suffering is divided into four aspects.

1. Cause
2. Origin
3. Full development
4. Circumstantial factors

Talking about karma law refers to the cause, the seed and circumstantial factors such as sun, water and so forth...

The third noble truth, the truth of the cessation of suffering is divided into four aspects.

1. Cessation
2. Peace
3. Blissfulness
4. Complete eradication

The fourth noble truth, the truth of the path leading to the cessation of suffering is divided into four aspects.

1. Path (Tib. Lam)
2. Awareness (Tib. Rigpa) *but not the meaning usually given in Dzogchen.*
3. Actualisation
4. Renouncement

This whole set of truths, including the Four Noble Truths and the sixteen smaller ones build the entrance's door into the Shravakas' vehicle. They all enable us to completely free ourselves from this cyclic existence, from Samsara. They do not enable us to realize the omniscient state of a Buddha, but rather to attain at least this state called "moksha", which means total liberation from any kind of suffering.

Nevertheless, even if these Four Noble Truths are more specific to the Shravakas' path, they still are the groundwork of any Buddhist practitioner. They should not be regarded with despise. On the hearers' path, Buddha spent much time teaching about renouncement. Even at the level of Vajrayana, it would be impossible to properly practise if this sense of renouncement was missing. The following Tibetan saying perfectly illustrates what is meant «Practising Mahamudra or Dzogchen without renouncement is practising like a fool ».

2. View (Tib. Tava)

The aim is here to realize the person's non-self.

The non-self of persons involves that a certain work should be done on the gross aggregates, specifically on the aggregates of physical body and on consciousness at its most superficial level. We are not talking about consciousness at its subtle level, whose essence is Clear Light. This physical aggregate has non-self existence, since, if we pulled away each part of the body, as we would, for example, take apart each petal of a flower, one after the other, then we would not be able to find any self within the body. The body can not be found anywhere. Where is the basis of "my body" ? We cut the ground from under our feet. We first take away a first identification basis of the "I" concept that is conveyed by the physical body.

Similarly, when we part the constituting elements of the aggregates building our sensations, perceptions, thoughts, our different kinds of sensorial consciousness and the mental consciousness itself, we come to the conclusion that, what seemed to be a reality, has indeed non-self existence.

The identification mental ground of the "I" concept is being pulled away. By breaking up the physical support into its component parts, we can notice that there is nothing existing within through itself of what we had experienced as possessing an intrinsic reality.

In the same way, with regard to feelings and perceptions, there is no more ground to the "mine" concept. Moreover, this concept of "I" can not exist neither outside the body, nor outside the thoughts, but if it existed there, so what would it be made of? Hence, the "I", deprived of any kind of support, "is falling down". There is one part of the experience that consists of "not finding" (Tib. Minyedpa). We pull away, one after the other, all the usual identification supports. By repeating this exercise many times, we can attain a realization of the non-self.

This point is a major one because the concept of «I», «Mine» or property really drives us in the Samsara, propelling us endlessly from one life into another. The only way to delete this distorted concept of "I", which is continuously feeding the Samsara, is to discover, through more or less analytical means, its lack of reality. This is the way Shravakas work on the non-self of persons. Through this understanding it is therefore possible to put an end to Samsara and to experience the extinguishing of suffering.

The following quotation by Candrakirti helps us better understand what we have just said: « At first, the "I" concept is being created and from that point, like its own shadow is the notion of "mine" or property being automatically developed. This sense of property spreads out to give birth to the concepts of "my " body, "my" head, "my" thoughts, "my" ideas, "my" feelings. Gradually, it is widely extending to encompass larger fields like "my parents", "my country", "my mountains" ».

We are totally trapped in the snares by which Samsara is driven. The hearers show a great practical intelligence through applying the precepts of Buddha. The truth of suffering must be recognized. They spend much time contemplating this aspect. Then, they try to know what is the cause of suffering. The cause of suffering is this notion of "I". As soon as this concept of "I" appears, everything is being distorted. Thus arises the origin of the problem. Everything must be done to recognize this lack of "I". There are many ways to proceed. Firstly through the analytical approach which consists of parting all components of that gross physical body or of the four aggregates, namely feelings, perceptions, thoughts or mental consciousness.

Through investigating, we can notice that "I" does not make "one" with the aggregates. This "I" does not make "one" with the head, and so forth in regard to perceptions, consciousness, etc. Nevertheless, it is not possible to say that this notion of "I" be completely unacquainted to the aggregates. If it was so, there would be no identification to the "I" concept, to the body and thus it would not be possible to think about perceptions. Therefore, this "I" concept is neither making "one", nor being "different". This leads us to experience "not finding". From this "not finding" experience, there is a space emerging, an opening up, whereby the lack of any "I" can be discovered. The hearer initially focuses on the absence of "I". As a result, he would be able to realize the great peace. Since there is no trace of "I", there is no chance for kleshas, contaminated activities and thus for suffering to arise.

To explore the person's non-self, the Shravaka has got three strings on his bow:

1. Textual quotations

The Shravaka relies on the scriptures relating to the words of Sakyamuni Buddha, whereby the absence of "I" is clearly presented, namely the non-self.

2. Power of examples

Through examples we can use the eight metaphors concerning delusion to explain the non-existence of the phenomena in general. These are like a dream, an echo, a mirage, a magical illusion, an optical illusion, a moonlight reflecting on water, a celestial gandharva city, an appearance or a ghost.

3. Power of reasoning

With the power of reasoning and analysing, the purpose is to reach out to the certainty of the non-existence of a self through considering the "one" and the "different". We have to find out, on the outer and inner level, whether this "I" makes "one" with one of the five aggregates: the aggregates of physical body, feelings, perceptions, thoughts or mental consciousness. The result of this investigation is not to find anything. Then, we have to investigate by seeking from the opposite way: is this "I" unacquainted to these five aggregates? How would it be possible to conceive the "I" concept if body, feelings, perceptions, thoughts or mental consciousness were not interacting? The "I" concept can not be unacquainted to the aggregates and at the same time it can not be found in them. Actually, this experience of certainty can not be gained only through investigation, which is merely a support. To really experience what is the absence of "I", we have to practise meditation.

It is important to analyse, but even more important is to practise meditation in silence. The different reasoning, the eight examples regarding the illusory reality and the textual quotations can help us. But if we merely satisfy ourselves with this kind of practise, it will lead us to the same kind of jest that made Gorampa Seunam Sengue, a great Sakyapa master, when he said: «When you are investigating on the "I", you come to the conclusion that "I" does not exist. As opposed to that, when you are stung by a needle, you shout: Ouch! Ouch! Ouch! ».

Drawing the lesson of this jest makes us understand that we have to learn how to meditate properly, so that once we have reached the conclusion of the non-existence of "I" and we have closed our book, we will see what occurs if a needle happens to sting us...

The Shravakas merely realize the person's non-self. They do not realize the non-self of phenomena. The philosophical schools to which the Shravakas belong stand for the idea that on a gross level, there is nothing existing in itself. For example, a flower has non-self-existence since there is nothing left, once you have pulled away all its petals, one after the other. And so it is similarly on a mental level. Nevertheless, both on a subtle and tangible level, the Shravakas do accept the atomic reality. They consider that it does exist in an absolute way. According to them, the tangible reality, the matter would not be able to arise if this atomic reality did not exist on an absolute level. They are convinced that the atomic reality really exists. And so it is similarly on a mental level. For sure is it possible, on a gross level, to part a moment of consciousness, but on an infinitely subtle level, when we reach the so-called 1/65th instant, the 65th part of this moment of consciousness, which represents the time needed to snap one's fingers, is seen as being self-existing. Therefore, the hearers can not attain the realization of the non-self of phenomena, since they do accept, whether on the tangible or mental level, the view of an indestructible reality, namely, the atomic reality as well as the reality of the finest moment of consciousness. As opposed to Bodhisattvas, Shravakas can not attain the realization of the non-self of phenomena, which, however, do not exist, even on an atomic level.

It is important to think deeply by ourselves, rather than by proxy, about the reality of the non-self of phenomena through studying sermons and treatises, then analysing, and finally through meditating. Shantideva said that merely questioning about the existence of "I" (is there any "I" or is it absent?) generally considered as a certainty, can reduce the power of desire, aversion-anger, kleshas and passions.

If this kind of result can be achieved by this mere questioning, how great would it be then if we realized the absence of "I"? When we are really experiencing this lack of "I", we can put an end to fleshes and reabsorb karma.

Regarding people who can not yet practice meditation, merely reading sermons or commentaries of the Buddha sermons, and investigating can lead them to the certainty that this "I" does not exist. This may happen even if there is a big difference between this experience and the one we can gain through meditating in complete silence, whereby we openly contemplate this lack of "I". Someone who has just entered the path and merely tries to make clear in his mind through reading and studying may intellectually come to the conclusion that "I" does not exist. In Tibet, in the 14th century, Tsongkhapa, who had gained a very high level of knowledge, taught his disciples about the reality of the non-self of persons and phenomena relying on the Buddha's quotations and on commentaries written by other masters or even on Rigpa, the power of reasoning and on syllogisms. Tsongkhapa was endowed with such a convincing power and eloquence, and his disciples were granted with such listening and concentration abilities, that some of them, even though they had achieved a high level of knowledge, had to check that they were still really existing by putting their hands on their body, because they were beginning to doubt. They were doing, what sometimes is called, a negative experience of the absolute or "dikta" in Tibetan, and they were scared. For such disciples, the power of kleshas was obviously breaking down by itself. There was no need struggling and saying: «I have to be a good person, I have to let go of attachment ».

3. The ethic (Tib. Tsültrim)

The ethic of hearers entails the upholding of any of the sets of vows aiming at individual liberation (Skt. Pratimoksha, Tib. Sosor Tharpa). By upholding the ethic that enables practitioners to remedy to the body' dysfunction, speech and mind, it is then possible for them by means of cultivating concentration and wisdom to gain liberation.

Five categories of vows

1. Quintuple ethic for laymen
2. Quintuple ethic for laywomen
3. Thirty-six vows for novice monks and nuns
4. Complete vows for bhiksus and bhiksunis
5. Nyung-Ne vows and fastening practice

1. Quintuple ethic for laymen

With respect to laypeople, there are five vows: no killing, no lying, no stealing, no sexual misconduct, no taking any toxic substances. Even if only one vow is taken, one becomes a lay practitioner. It is possible to uphold only one vow, but with full commitment. Or it is possible to take two or three vows among the five lay vows, and become a part lay practitioner. Taking all of them enables us to become a full lay practitioner.

2. Quintuple ethic for laywomen

The ethic for laywomen is exactly the same than for laymen.

3. Thirty six vows for novice monks and nuns

There are thirty-six vows of novice monks and nuns. Before being ordained as novice nuns and during their probation time, women must uphold ten root precepts during two years.

4. Complete vows for bhiksus and bhiksunis

In the case of fully ordained monks and nuns (Pal. Bhiksu and Bhiksuni), there are two hundreds and fifty-three vows for monks and three hundreds and sixty-four vows for nuns.

5. Nyung-Ne vows and fastening practice

In respect to Nyung-Ne vows and the Mahayana

fastening's practice, there are eight vows to uphold during twenty-four hours, or a period of time to be otherwise determined:

– there are four ground vows: no killing, no stealing, no lying, and full chastity during the given time.

– there are four complementary vows: no drinking of any alcoholic beverages, no sitting on a high seat, no eating after lunch time up to the following morning by sunrise, avoiding any kind of shallow deeds, like dancing, singing, dressing up and so forth ...

As we can see, these different commitments are quite numerous, but in their very essence, they are all about renouncement. If we accept renouncing, these vows can be very easily upheld. If we hold things by their roots, all the other parts such as branches or leaves are very easily taking place. Instead, if we hold things by their branches, then we spend our time struggling.

On the hearers' path, the living heart of the practice is based on this sense of renouncement and on the Four Noble Truths, which are constantly present in the mind of the practitioner.

On the Bodhisattvas' path, the living heart of the practice consists of deepening the experience of Bodhicitta and contemplating emptiness, which involves meditating on the causal pattern, nowadays also called interdependence origination and what Buddha named the twelve causes of interdependence.

On the path of secret mantras or Vajrayana, the living heart of the practice consists of upholding samayas or commitments and stabilizing the mind in Rigpa, what is referred to in Dzogchen, as being in a state of pure mindfulness and wisdom. Once engaged in the Hinayana, if the practitioner succeeds in developing renouncement, or once engaged in the Mahayana, if the practitioner cultivates Bodhicitta and meditates on the cause pattern, or once engaged in the Vajrayana, if the practitioner perfectly upholds his commitments and stabilizes his or her mind in Rigpa, then we can say that the innermost essence of the practise is accomplished.

4. The meditation (Tib. Gompa)

On the one hand, meditation practised by hearers consists of calm abiding or mental quiescence (Skt. Samatha, Tib. Shine), which means resting in a peaceful state. There are nine stages to gain samatha, to rest the mind, pacify it and calm it down.

On the other hand, this meditation practice means developing superior seeing (Skt. Vipasyana, Tib. Lhaktong), namely developing profound insight into the sixteen small truths or subdivisions of the Four Noble Truths. This meditation practice enables us to nourish the fire of lhaktong.

Nine stages of samatha

1. First stage: Focussing

According to the Tibetan expression, resting the mind means "resting while guiding". In English, we could translate by "focussing". In regard to the Vajrayana context, this focussing is occurring at the time of Kyerim, while meditating on the yidam or on the seed-syllable (Skt. Bija). We are focussing our whole attention on this letter, for example Om or Houng, or on the yidam itself. The purpose is resting our mind while guiding it.

2. Second stage: Continuous focussing

Here it deals with sustained focussing, literally translated from Tibetan by "continuous focussing". As a matter of fact, focussing has to be, not only clear, but also unbroken, without any distraction.

3. Third stage: Restored focussing

Focussing can be restored as well as attention when it has been broken by outer incentives like sounds, visual forms or by inner incentives like thoughts. This capacity of attention may be diverted but it can be strengthened again, and hence being re-directed to the focal support and so restore the focussing. It is literally translated from Tibetan by "mended focussing, or patched up focussing".

4. Fourth stage: Tight focussing

Even if there are some outer or inner incentives to divert his practice, the practitioner is not being distracted very long, but instead capable to draw back his attention swiftly to his focal support. In the previous stage, diversion has really occurred and settled, whereas at this fourth stage, distraction may appear but it will have less chance to last.

5. Fifth stage: Controlling

Once this stage is reached, the mental starts to really calm down. It becomes smooth, peaceful and tamed. It begins to control its passions, such as desire, attachment it had been unable to tame up to this stage. But at this point of the training, the different disturbing elements are subjugated.

6. Sixth stage: Pacifying

The state of peace that is established within ourselves can progressively lead to pacifying the more and more subtle waves of thoughts. Thoughts appear first like powerful strong waves, big rollers, which gradually slow and calm down, becoming like tiny waves.

7. Seventh stage: Total pacification

At this stage of meditation practice, the subtlest movements of thoughts have been pacified.

8. Eighth stage: Unifying

During the previous stages, it was still necessary to give some energy for maintaining a continuous concentration. Here a slight effort is enough to keep the attention flow and thus the enhanced experience of peacefulness. Unifying means that there is no longer any kind of splitting between mind, on one hand, and method, on the other hand, which corresponds to the focussing ability used by the mind. Mind and technical method begin to make one, to operate as a single man, in union. Only a slight effort is needed within our sustained attention to keep focussing so that the calming and pacifying experience can last, spread and stabilize.

9. Ninth stage: Meditation absorption

This last stage is called meditation absorption, or meditative concentration, or perfect equanimity (Skt. Samadhi, Tib. ting nye zin) and arises spontaneously, from within, naturally. At this point of the practice, problems related to dullness or agitation that used to arise previously have been completely eradicated. While practising a certain kind of insight, there may be a time, during which we experience sleepiness or apathy, as if we were sinking. Clarity is lost. We are getting bogged down and stuck. Once this ninth and last stage has been reached, sleepiness does not arise any longer. When we are quite involved and connected to our five senses in regard to the world and other people, a certain kind of agitation is arising, but at this stage, it has completely disappeared.

At this highest stage, we reach what is called meditative absorption that exists in a natural state that is spontaneously present. It is part of our true nature, our Buddha nature. This progressive way through the different stages implies efforts, sustained attention and enables us to gain a state that has been already here since the origin and for which there is no need to strive.

Metaphors related to the nine Samatha stages

The first three samatha stages are depicted as a waterfall, still very powerful. The following three stages look rather like a river's stream that has reached the flat plain, smoothly snaking its way through the countryside. The last three stages are compared to the ocean with its waves. Even if waves are still rising, they easily vanish into the ocean.

These nine samatha stages, whose purpose is to calm down our mental, are absolutely essential. We can apply them on a «worldly» level, merely for developing concentration without switching into superior seeing, what Buddhists call vipasyana.

Vipasyana is transcending the world. It is no longer a concentration or mental pacifying exercise, but rather attaining profound insight, a first understanding of the absolute that is conveyed by the lack of self.

To finish this presentation of shine in nine stages, let's refer to Mipam Rinpoche, who declared that it is absolutely possible to practice samatha within Dzogchen. This method can be used to pacify the mental. There is no need being a spiritual person longing for absolute knowledge to use this method of mental pacification, but nevertheless this method can also be practiced in the light of Dzogchen.

Samatha should not be underestimated even if the way of practising in Dzogchen does not fully rely on this method, as it is usually explained.

5. The conduct (Tib. Chödpa)

The conduct consists of getting the twelve learning qualities. Shravakas, particularly at the time of Buddha and during the following centuries, have generally been monks or novices, but never laypeople. In this vehicle, when it comes to conduct, most of the time it implies the behaviour of monks, nuns and novices.

Monks's or novices's way of life:

To earn their living, they do not work in fields like lay people, but they usually beg. They have to content themselves with alms.

Monks's or novices's place of residence:

They have to settle down in a place convenient for meditation. They should not run about like goats or dogs.

Monks's or novices's clothes:

They are dressed in rags. They should collect clothes that have been thrown away by laypeople, then wash and mend them before dyeing them in ochre or maroon. Clothes should be made up of cast-offs. Novices and monks wear the three dharma clothes. The bottom part is maroon and the two top parts are made up with yellow patched pieces.

Special features of the place of residence:

It should be remote (Tib. Gompa) outside any village and convenient for meditation. Originally, monks and nuns have no houses, but merely a large tree endowed with sufficiently large foliage to protect them from rain or sun, at the foot of which they can meditate.

Body posture:

Practitioners are mostly sitting. Even in the middle of the night, they wake up and sit to practise meditation in the accurate sitting posture.

6. The result (Tib. Drebu)

The result of all these practices is easily gained. It looks like a meal: preparing the food requires efforts but eating is very easy.

For Shravakas, fruition entails four phases:

1. Entering the mind's stream;
2. Coming back through one rebirth;
3. Not being reborn;
4. Gaining the Arhat state of total liberation from Samsara, without any possible return.

When we get closer into analysing, fruition can be presented through eight parts, since each stage can be divided into two phases. One phase refers to "entering" and the resulting one to "abiding in fruition". All together it makes eight phases.

For example, the first stage called "entering the stream" is the accessing phase: we put one foot into the river. Then we are in the phase of "abiding in fruition", which means that we are fully immersed in the river.

Through the power of the view, the ability to deeply investigate and realize the non-self of persons, thanks to meditating shine and lhaktong, it is possible to totally dismantle this machinery that feeds Samsara, and thus to get freed from it. On the shravakayana path, there are three major points to remember: renouncement, contemplation upon the Four Noble Truths and contemplation upon the person's non-self.

Today without moving a single toe from our chair, we have been through the whole Shravakas' path. Tomorrow still comfortably sitting here, we will learn about the path of Pratyekabuddhas. This first vehicle of the Shravakas is one of the three rising vehicles through emanations.

Conclusion

The purpose of this presentation of the nine Yana by stages is to lead us to making up our mind. This is similar to a menu carte. We can choose among these paths which one will best suit us. It could be for instance the Shravakas' path which implies to really invest our spiritual energy, since realization is not gained easily. If we feel more inspired by the Bodhisattvas' path, we will have to develop Bodhicitta, the Heart of Enlightenment. It is up to us to decide which of these nine paths will best match our motivation.

Looking at these nine paths, is like going into a five-star restaurant offering an extraordinary choice of dishes, where all different kinds of food can be selected, from the entire world: Asiatic food, Continental food, French cuisine and so forth. We can choose between wine, mineral water, vegetarian or non-vegetarian dishes and so forth.

With the first two vehicles, the rising vehicle through emanations and the knowledge vehicle through asceticism, we are still having vegetarian food. But when it comes to the vehicle of skilful transcending means, especially with respect to Dzogchen, there, we can spend the night in a night club, eating meat, drinking alcohol and so forth . . . the three postures, the three visions, dancing and singing all night long. But do not worry! It is all about vajra songs and dances, no disco!

Pratyekabuddhayana, the path of the "self-Buddha"

The proper state of mind to receive teachings

To listen to teachings, it is important to be in a proper state of mind. We have to generate the Bodhicitta, which means developing a wide thinking, opening up our heart towards all beings, which is typical of Bodhisattvas engaged in Mahayana. But at the same time, we also have to develop the essence of Vajrayana, namely pure vision thanks to the immense diversity of the skilful means available to practitioners.

While presenting the gradual path of the nine vehicles, we are able to "collect", literally translated from Tibetan, that means essentialise the whole enligthened thought by the Hinayana, Mahayana and Vajrayana.

The first three vehicles regarding sutras, the shravakayana, the pratyekabuddhayana and the bodhisattvayana are «rising vehicles through emanations». As a matter of fact, they enable through instructions on sustained attention, calm abiding and superior seeing to liberate beings from the different states resulting from the six realms of rebirth, from the emotional poisons (Skt. Klesha) and the contaminated karma.

The outer tantras, the kriya, charya and yoga tantras, are the "knowledge vehicles through asceticism", or through discipline.

The inner tantras, the Maha, Anu and Ati yoga, are three upper vehicles which enable «transcending through skilful means». They can produce a kind of alchemical process that leads the five poisons back to their innermost essence, being experienced as they truly are, namely the five original wisdoms.

The first of these vehicles which "enable rising through emanations" is the vehicle of the Shravakas: it is meant for disciples with lower faculties. The second vehicle of Pratyekabuddhas or "self-Buddhas" is meant for disciples with medium faculties. The third vehicle of Mahayana is meant for disciples with upper faculties.

The path of the "self-Buddha"

The path of "self-Buddhas" is very similar to the path of Shravakas. The realization we may gained through this path is very close to the one of the Shravakas. "self-Buddhas" learns to develop the power of wishing prayers (Tib. Mönlam), which mostly differentiate them from the hearers. But apart from that aspect, they have many common points.

In their previous lives, "self-Buddhas" had wished not to be depending on a spiritual master in the present lifetime (Tib. Lopön/Lama), but instead, through the mere power of contemplation upon the twelve links of interdependence origination, to be able to realize the non-self of persons as well as partially — Bodhisattvas do realize it totally — the non-self of phenomena. They do not attain yet realization of the emptiness of consciousness itself.

A spiritual desert

We have to emphasize that "self-Buddhas" appear at a time that looks rather like a spiritual desert. Through the mere power of past prayers and wishes such as « May I appear at a time when teaching will have disappeared» and without being dependent on a guru, thus, they are able to go through this transitional spiritual time which is the lapse between the end of a teaching and a new era.

By this way, they can accomplish fruition which is to put an end to their life in Samsara.

Etymology

"self-Buddhas" (Skt. Pratyekabuddha, Tib. Rang Gyal) are great heart-minded beings who had wished to appear at a period of time when the Buddha's teachings have completely disappeared from earth. They do not rely on a teacher, but through their previous prayers, they have developed such a spiritual power that they can become solitary practitioners or solitary realizers. Therefore they are named "self-buddhas". Sakyamuni Buddha himself declared that during these lapses of spiritual desert when there is no Buddha appearing and when Arhats have entered into the realm of Great Peace, "self-Buddhas" do appear thanks to the power of their past prayers and so succeed to attain essential primordial wisdom (Skt. Jnana, Tib. Yeshe) through their contemplation upon the twelve links of interdependent origination.

The six linking points

1. Entrance's door (Tib. Jugo)

The entrance's door of the Pratyekabuddhas consists of the twelve links of interdependent origination existing both at outer and inner level.

"self-Buddhas" explore by themselves through contemplating again and again on this chain of the twelve interdependent links. Hence, they can achieve the first form of enlightened awareness (Tib. Sherab), then the second one resulting from reflecting and analyzing that leads them to a certainty (Tib. Nge She). From that point, they move to the third step, even more crucial that is meditation (Tib. Gompa).

The twelve links of interdependent origination at an outer level

Considering the twelve links of interdependent origination

at an outer level, means to relate them to the outer phenomena. The twelve links are subdivided into six links related to cause, and into six links related to fruition or result.

Causes and conditions

While reflecting on the twelve links of interdependent origination (Skt. Nidana, Tib. Tendrel) at an outer level, the first arising idea is concerning causality that we can easily and openly observe: the seed is the cause, which gives birth to the sprout, which gives birth to the shoot, which gives birth to the stem, which gives flowers and then fruits. This phenomenon is the result of the mere observation at an outer level.

Six links are related to causes and six links are related to conditions. In the concrete case of a seed we sew, the conditions are the five elements: earth, water, fire, wind and space. The sixth element is time. At the outer level, all the phenomena belonging to the objective reality are subjected to the law of karma. These phenomena, whatever they are, a flower, a plant or whatsoever... can not appear by themselves. They depend on causes and conditions which are considered as allies. All these factors together allow the appearing and disappearing of phenomena.

At a deeper level, the practitioner becomes more familiar with the interdependent origination and with the links binding phenomena in the way they manifest, which is fleeting and impermanent.

Even more deeply, the practitioner experiences the non-self of phenomena.

Phenomena are no created since their existence depends on causes and conditions. They are interdependent.

The twelve links of interdependence origination at an inner level

As far as the twelve links of interdependence origination are concerned at an inner level, it is about the receptacle, all living beings, including human beings as well as animals and insects. The "self-Buddhas" is orienting his or her contemplation upon the twelve links of interdependence origination in relation to all living beings. By this way, he or she will, at first place, attain the realization of the non-self of persons.

Starting from cause to result, we can find the following links: the first one is ignorance (1), referring to misunderstanding, not knowing or distorted knowledge. From ignorance appear formations (2) (Skt. Samskara, Tib. Dü Dje). From those formations appear the five sensory perceptions and the mental consciousness (3) which are flawed with the "I" concept. From this consciousness manifest name and form (4). From there appear sensory and mental organs, called the six main organ locations (5). From these organs appears contact (6). From contact emerges feeling (7), from feeling appears craving (8), from craving arises grasping (9), from grasping appears becoming (10) from becoming emerges birth (11), from birth appear old age and death (12).

Through the power of the prayer they made in their previous lifetimes that tells: « May I be born in a time when there are neither Buddhas nor Arhats and when the Baghavan's teaching will have completely disappeared », the Pratyekabuddhas, endowed with a certain spiritual maturity as they are on an advanced path, will awaken within themselves the contemplation of the twelve links. Contemplation can begin when they see a bone or go to cemeteries, as there were so many in ancient India. They will not necessary see a corpse, but merely a white bone they can use as a support for their contemplation and reflection. As they feel concerned, they start then wondering, just as Buddha himself did. Where does the bone come from? The bone appeared because someone is dead, death can happen only because birth has occurred, birth can occur only because there has been becoming. Thus it is possible to trace these connections all the way back to the mainspring, which is ignorance. From there arise many questions: what is the nature of ignorance, of this not knowing? What makes it so powerful to produce such a huge interrelated succession of phenomena? Hence, they understand that ignorance comes from ego-clinging, the clinging to a truly illusory «I». They become aware that realizing the non-self of persons can un-knot this chain. Like hearers, they understand that ego-clinging produces Samsara and once we will stop this ego-clinging, the whole Samsara would be consequently liberated. As soon as ignorance does not exist any more, "samskaras" disappear as well as all the subsequent links, thus completely undoing the chain. These practitioners meditate this way again and again, following the whole cycle from cause to result, examining each link. Then reversing the order of their meditation from result to cause to trace the whole chain back, and so forth until they attain the perfect realization of the non-self of persons.

The twelve links of this chain of interdependence origination are automatically related to three main aspects: kleshas or disturbing emotions, karmas or contaminated actions, and suffering.

Which of the twelve links are related to kleshas?

Ignorance (1), craving (8) and grasping (9).

Which of the twelve links are related to contaminated karmas?

Formations (2) and becoming (10).

Which of the twelve links are related to suffering?

The seven remaining links are related to suffering.

The chain of the twelve interdependent links within three lifetimes

It is said that this chain is spreading over three lifetimes in order to loop the loop.

Ignorance (1) and formations (2) come from a past lifetime.

From the six consciousness (3) up to becoming (10), which is occurring at the time of death, present lifetime is concerned.

Birth (11) and "old age and death" (12) occur in the next lifetime.

Pratyekabuddhas do not contemplate the six small truths (cf. page 30) as Shravakas do. Their particularity is to contemplate the twelve links of interdependence origination which lead them to a high level of realization, to primordial wisdom.

2. View (Tib. Tava)

Pratyekabuddhas realize the non-self of persons as Shravakas do. However, Shravakas only realize the non-self of persons without considering the non-self of phenomena, since they do accept the existence of atom at a physical level, and at a mental level they also approve the existence of infinitely subtle moments of consciousness.

"self-Buddhas" go a step further since they attain half a realization of the non-self of phenomena through realizing the non-self of atoms. According to them, there is non-self existing tangible atomic reality, whereas Shravakas do think it is self-existing. "self-Buddhas" succeed to understand that atoms, regarded as "indivisible and indestructible" can be divided to such a point of no created dimension. Therefore, "self-Buddhas" become aware of emptiness and of the non-self of phenomena related to the atomic reality. But they do not attain this realization regarding mental reality. They still keep on thinking that infinitely subtle moments of consciousness are self existing. As a result they do not attain the whole understanding and realization of the non-self, whereas Bodhisattvas do.

"self-Buddhas" consider that the four elements composing the tangible reality at the outer level or the physical aggregate at the inner level, are not self-existing. Furthermore, they consider that the atomic reality at an infinite subtle level is not self-existing. They are also aware that there is still this dualistic pattern of subject/object, of someone grasping (Tib. Dzinpa) and something being grasped (Tib. Zungpa). Through contemplating the twelve links of interdependence origination, they become aware that this reality of the object, regarded as tangible, has no foundation.

It is logical to think that without this embryo of consciousness, it would be impossible to get to know anything. According to "self-buddhas", when we trace back to its shortest and subtlest instants, the subject/consciousness substantially exists. It has got a reality.

"self-Buddhas" hold on to the following conviction: « If consciousness did not exist, nothing could be known and it would be absurd ». To state that nothing can be known, a consciousness is needed, thus, a consciousness must exist. By this way, this conviction prevents the "self-Buddhas" from moving forward and realizing the non-self of phenomena, as do Bodhisattvas realize it."self-Buddhas" experience the objective reality as illusory existing (cf. the eight metaphors regarding illusion page 33). At the subtlest level of consciousness, they think consciousness is endowed with a certain reality. This aspect prevents them from fully realizing the non-self of phenomena. They only attain half a realization, as the Tibetan expression tells. "self-Buddhas" only have a realization and a half of the non-self.

3. Ethic (Tib. Tsültrim)

The ethic of the "self-Buddhas" is the one of the Shravakas akin.

4. Meditation (Tib. Gompa)

As far as "self-Buddhas" are concerned, meditation exclusively consists of contemplating the twelve links of interdependence origination from cause to result and in the reverse order from result to cause, which lead them to realizing the Four Noble Truths.

The Four Noble Truths under the light of the twelve links of interdependence origination

1. Understanding the first two noble truths from cause to result.

When this contemplation is carried out in the original order from cause to result, namely from ignorance up to old age and death, it concerns the truth of suffering and the truth of the origin of suffering.

2. Understanding the first two noble truths from result to cause.

When "self-Buddhas" contemplate the twelve links of interdependence origination in the reverse order, from result to cause, they come to reflect upon the two other truths, namely the truth of the eightfold path and the truth of the cessation of suffering.

They succeeded in fully permeating these Four Noble Truths through merely considering, for example, as support to their meditation, the last link among the twelve, that is to say old age and death. Through understanding the depths of this truth, they pinpoint the truth of suffering. Afterwards, they ask the same question that the prince Gautama himself asked: « Where do old age and death come from? ». They are the result from birth, corresponding to the truth of the origin of suffering. Next step leads them to think that, if we put an end to birth, it will bring with it the extinction of old age, death and suffering. From this point they reach to a true intuitive sense of what is the cessation of suffering.

Suffering arising and eliminating

Two stages are presented here: the first one is the elimination of suffering and the second one is the arising of suffering.

"self-Buddhas" are able to get familiar with the truth of the origin of suffering merely through contemplating the twelve-link process: from ignorance arise formations, from formations appear consciousness and so forth up to old age and death. While understanding the truth of the origin of suffering, they understand the truth of the path leading to the extinction of suffering.

If we cut through the first link of ignorance, as a result all Samskaras or formations will also disappear since they have no more support and thus, if Samskaras have lost their support, consciousness themselves will also lose their support, and so forth up to the final link. If the first link collapse, so do all other links, one after the other, like a house of cards.

By this way, "self-Buddhas" realize the truth of the path that leads to the extinction of suffering. The truth of the path consists of breaking down self-grasping and permeating non-self. No more support for Kleshas, no more support for conflicting emotions, no more support for contaminated activities. The aim is to thwart the arising of suffering. Through sustained and repeated contemplation of the twelve links in their appearing and eliminating process can "self-Buddhas" deeply permeate the Buddha's words which consist of the four truths of noble beings, namely those who have realized direct vision of the absolute reality.

Unlike Shravakas who listen and receive teachings from a master, "self-buddhas", without depending on a guru and through the mere power of their past prayers which drive them forward and give them the energy and strength to progress on their own path, are immediately concerned by the twelve-link process of interdependence origination and by the means to cut it through, as well as by the four truths of noble beings.

5. Conduct (Tib. Chödpa)

Mudra, a profound sacred gesture

Even if they practise on their own, "self-Buddhas" begin, at a given time, to have disciples. To communicate their teachings, "self-Buddhas" do not use the speech but they express themselves through different symbolic body movements called "mudra". Sometimes the whole body may be involved in this symbolic expression (Tib. Da). People who have then become their disciples recognize themselves in the "self-Buddhas" thanks to the teachings expressed by symbolic body gestures. And they start to practise.

This Buddha nature can be awakened either within the shravakayana, or within the pratyekabuddhayana through the realization of the Four Noble Truths and not through the precepts relevant to Bodhisattvas. The different body expressions of the realized "self-Buddhas" enable disciples to decipher the teaching upon the ten virtuous deeds or upon the Four Noble Truths or the twelve links of interdependence origination although no word needs to be spoken.

In the Abhisamayalankara, which is one of the five great treatises by Maitreya, the future Buddha says: « When he teaches on his turn, the "self-Buddhas" expresses himself a lot with his body ».

Deer Park

A teaching place located near the present city of Sarnath in India, Deer Park was a forest of does, deers and cervidaes, where Buddha turned for the first time the Dharma wheel. This is a high place of spiritual practices of our fortunate time whereby the historical Buddha himself taught, as well as many other Buddhas of previous and former kalpas as they appeared in supreme Nirmanakaya. During the transitory time when there were no more manifested Buddhas, "self-Buddhas" appeared there and became later Arhats. This is a very special site, where many extraordinary events took place. Once they have become Arhats, "self-Buddhas" do not leave their body by ordinary ways. Out of their body, which first rises up in the air, water flows, flames appear as well as rains of pearls (Tib. Ringsel). These relics of small pearls flowing out from the body of realized beings like rains of blessings have so often covered up Deer Park!

Such phenomena belong to the activity, to the behaviour of "self-Buddhas" when they reach out Nirvana. They explain how, even at their body level, such supernatural, marvellous phenomena occur, and how their body loose their material appearance and turn into a shower of ringsel.

Similar events happened a few decades ago as Tibetan people lost their ground and had to flee, at the time of the 16th Karmapa Rangdjoung Rigpe Dordje, in the fifties. Some of these great masters went into exile to Taiwan, the Formosa Island. Some Chinese people living there witnessed similar events. They tell how great masters rose up into the sky, how water flew and then flames spurted out of their body. It may sound contradictory since it is said that "self-Buddhas" appear in times of spiritual desert, but nevertheless it is true that they also may happen during other eras. This is what people could see and witnessed with their own eyes.

6. Result (Tib. Drebu)

Two types of Pratyekabuddhas

Pratyekabuddhas similar to rhinoceros

Pratyekabuddhas granted with especially sharp faculties are completely autonomous and self-sufficient and hold rather aloof from others, a little bit rhinoceros alike and solitary realize fruition.

Pratyekabuddhas similar to parrots

Pratyekabuddhas granted with coarser faculties, who are more socializing, parrots alike, are looking for company and realize fruition with others.

Differences and similarities between Pratyekabuddhas and Shravakas.

There are many similarities between hearers and "self-Buddhas" but important points make them different.

Differences

Pratyekabuddhas attain the realization of the non-self of phenomena in regard to objects, which is not the case for Shravakas.

For Pratyekabuddhas meditating means pursuing sustained contemplation upon the twelve links of interdependence origination, from cause to result and then in reverse order, which is not the case for Shravakas.

Pratyekabuddhas appear at a dark or gloomy era (Tib. Kalpa) when all Buddhist teachings have totally been lost without any single trace left.

Similarities

The common point of Shravakas and Pratyekabuddhas is the fundamental principle of renouncement, a strong conviction that Samsara has no foundation and deprived of any interest. This enables them to give birth to an inner deep aspiration, an acute longing for realizing liberation. Nonetheless both kinds of practitioners show a common limitation: they are too much centred to their individual realization.

Their lack of energy prevents them from being propelled up to the full Enlightenment of a Buddha.

It is important to understand how these so-called «lower» paths are working and what inner dynamics are driving them. Moreover, being inspired by them and trying to realize for ourselves as many qualities as possible required by both of these basic vehicles, is also a very essential task.

Mahayana, the path of Bodhisattvas

Patrul Rinpoche said that it is absolutely necessary to set the appropriate means which will enable us to attain full Enlightenment, and not doing so is a real defect within our practice.

Aspiration Bodhicitta and application Bodhicitta

Cultivating Bodhicitta enables us to move forwards to Enlightenment. Bodhicitta entails two aspects: the intention one, called aspiration Bodhicitta, and the action one, called application Bodhicitta. Bodhicitta is the main concept in Mahayana applied by Bodhisattvas committing themselves to serve the infinite multitude of beings and to free them all from Samsara.

Now that we are dealing with Mahayana, it is crucial to generate Bodhicitta, even if it is merely intentional. This makes the superiority of this path compared with the paths of hearers and "self-buddhas". It has nothing to do here with value judgement, but this method has really the power to propel us up to full Enlightenment.

Bodhicitta, the Heart of Enlightenment or in other words loving-kindness, hearted-generosity is meant for the infinite multitude of beings. It provides great mental and body well-being in the present lifetimes. Bodhicitta is an immense source of welfare and always brings positive and good things both in present and future time.

The last of the three rising vehicles through emanations

In this presentation of the nine yana put together into three major vehicles, Mahayana is the last one of the first set of three vehicles called «rising vehicles through emanations», otherwise literally translated from Tibetan by "freeing vehicles from samsaric worlds", or "freeing vehicles from kleshas", or even "freeing vehicles from contaminated karmas".

Meaning

What does the word Mahayana mean? Maha means "great" and Yana "vehicle". What makes it a "great" vehicle? It is a great vehicle because the corresponding path is higher than the two previous paths. The term «great vehicle» encompasses the whole Buddha's teachings based on the Sutras which emphasize the pre-eminence of the Bodhisattva ideal and of universal compassion over individual liberation.

The seven features of Mahayana

1. Space-like focusing

The first feature characterizing Mahayana is "space-like focusing". Such an insight is as vast as space when it comes to fully realizing the non-self of persons and phenomena, which is attained precisely by Bodhisattvas. Whereas Pratyekabuddhas attain partial realization, Bodhisattvas realize a global total view, what Buddha called the "non-self", thus it is becoming a space-like view. The word focusing should be understood as a zperception. It depicts the extraordinary vast quality of the perception of the non-self realization.

2. Great practice

The "great practice" is distinguishing the Bodhisattvas' path from those of hearers and "self-Buddhas". Hearers and "self-Buddha's" are certainly not selfish, but they merely plan to realize the cessation of suffering only for themselves, since they think they have not enough capacity and energy to attain full Enlightenment. Their practice is mainly driven by longing for personal achievement. Bodhisattvas will attain realization for themselves — since it is not possible to help others without being enlightened — as well as realization for all beings. Once they are realized, then they can help others to attain Enlightenment.

It is designated as a "great practice" since it is driven by these two kinds of aspirations and motivations: liberation of ourselves and liberation of others. This great practice implies great energy.

3. Great wisdom

As far as Bodhisattvas are concerned, it is referred to "great wisdom", why? Would it mean that Shravakas and Pratyekabuddhas are deprived of great wisdom? Not at all! As a matter of fact, Shravakas attain a realization of the non-self that is already relevant to great emptiness. As they realize the non-self of persons, they have already permeated the field of the absolute realization, what Buddha called "Great Emptiness" in the Prajnaparamita. This is even more appropriate for Pratyekabuddhas, as they have also half realized the non-self of phenomena. Shravakas and Pratyekabuddhas are endowed with great wisdom. However, why is that wisdom even greater concerning Bodhisattvas? It is an immense wisdom because it is completely nurtured by love and compassion, more accurately by "limitless loving-kindness", which is a specific experience of great compassion. This wisdom is enhanced by the fact that realization and perception of emptiness merge with the experience of great compassion and limitless loving-kindness for the infinite multitude of beings and living creatures. As this wisdom connected with the absolute is nurtured by love and compassion, it makes it more radiant and brighter than the wisdom achieved by the practitioners of the two previous Yana. Wisdom and love are in union. Both are making one and thus arises "great wisdom" (Tib. Yeshe Tchenpo).

4. Great energy

The fourth characteristic feature is "great energy". It is a kind of sustained energy (Skt. Virya) enhanced by perseverance and enthusiasm, and nurtured by joyfulness and liveliness. The energy spread out and provided by Bodhisattvas is much more immense than the one displayed by hearers and "self-Buddhas". The energy put into action by hearers and "self-Buddhas" merely aims at their own individual liberation without any other motivation.It is a short-termed energy.

Unlike them, a Bodhisattva spends his energy in a long-termed perspective and utters such following wishes: « As long as Samsara is not emptied of all beings living in confusion, I will stay here; I will never leave Samsara until this is achieved ». This loving connection is a real commitment. All endeavours are made to fully awaken ourselves and to enable others to awaken. Hence, it is not restricted to strive ourselves to get freed of conflicting emotions (Skt. Klesha) and reach out Nirvana, but it deals with all possible efforts carried out lifetimes after lifetimes to be fully enlightened, and so forth until all sentient beings also awaken to their true nature. It is a colossal energy spread out without restraint.

5. Expertise within skilful means

Through merely focusing on their individual liberation, hearers and "self-Buddhas" fall in a kind of extreme attitude called "the extreme of loss". The only aim of Shravakas and Pratyekabuddhas is to leave Samsara and to remain in peace. By this way, Shravakas and Pratyekabuddhas eventually come to a point, whereby they get bogged down and stuck in this peaceful state, they feel satisfied with. Unlike them, Bodhisattvas never sink into the extreme of peace nor into the extreme of Samsara, as they are doing their utmost to spread out the great wisdom of the absolute, which is the opposite of Samsara. They neither stay in Samsara, nor do they satisfy themselves with any achieved peaceful state. Therefore, it is said that Bodhisattvas never fall into the extreme of peace, nor into the extreme of Samsara.

Not falling into any of these extremes conveys expertise within skilful means.

6. Great realization

Realization means result. When Bodhisattvas reach the last bhumis among the ten bhumis of realization, they are moving on forward to attain full Enlightenment. They are about realizing all qualities of a fully realized Buddha. They are granted with the four bravery signs (Tib. Mi-jig-pa chi), which are typical of a fully enlightened Buddha mind manifested into Nirmanakaya.

Four bravery signs:

1. Certainty of never falling again into confusion.
2. Certainty of total elimination of veils and defilements.
3. Certainty of providing antidotes for the sake of others.
4. Certainty of showing others what has to be abandoned.

Buddha is also endowed with the following hundred and twelve signs:

Eighty minor signs:

Numerous signs of beauty, evidences of his perfect Enlightenment;

Thirty-two major signs:

Among the thirty-two major signs, there is, for example, the protuberance on the top of the head.

Those hundred and twelve signs convey this full Enlightenment, this "great realization" which can be attained only through the Bodhisattvas' path.

7. Great activities

The seventh characteristic feature related to "great activities" is developed by great Bodhisattvas and Buddhas, who are fully awakened, and thus able to care for the benefit of all beings. Those "great activities" entail three aspects.

8. Never stopping activity like an engine of a nuclear station

First aspect

Those "great activities" manifest spontaneously without any effort. Noble activities of Bodhisattvas are carried out through that immense compassion which has been generated lifetimes after lifetimes on the Mahayana path. It works like the engine of a nuclear station that never stops.

Second aspect

Those "great activities" perfectly adapt themselves to the different thinking ways and abilities of beings. Those activities are not carried out on an equal or unique manner, but they rather do appear in respond to the various numerous aspirations of beings.

Third aspect

As far as time is concerned those "great activities" have been unbroken. The commitment of the Bodhisattva is to stay in Samsara as long as there will be people left in confusion. The Bodhisattva declares: «As long as Samsara is not emptied of all beings living in confusion, I will stay here, I will never leave Samsara until this is achieved ».

Essence of Bodhisattvas

What is a bodhisattva? What is his essence?

A practitioner becomes a Bodhisattva through his realization of the non-self of persons and phenomena, through his realization of the absolute or in other words Great Emptiness, and through the power of sustained love and compassion that does not stop growing to benefit all beings.

Putting all this into action on a constant way and without any restraint is the innermost essence of a Bodhisattva.

Etymology

In Sanskrit, Bodhisattva means "Being of Enlightenment"

and in Tibetan is literally translated by "Hero of the Heart of Enlightenment". This word implies the notion of Enlightenment for oneself — since it is necessary to awaken our consciousness — as well as Enlightenment for others. The commitment is complete, even if it takes numerous kalpas, many cosmic eras, many lifetimes. Bodhisattvas never demoralize, but instead keep on moving along their brave path. They are warriors of Enlightenment since they are never discouraged and never feel careless or powerless.

Six linking points

1. Entrance's door (Tib. Jugo)

The entrance's door of Bodhisattvas is the understanding of the two following truths: the relative and the absolute ones.

Absolute truth conveys the essential and ultimate nature of all phenomena and relative truth refers to phenomena appearances. It is important to understand that relative truth is a dissembling truth because it conceals the absolute.

Why are the Four Noble Truths the foundations of this path leading to Enlightenment?

Within Hinayana, there are very strict behaviour rules which emphasize upon what has to be cultivated in practice and what has to be discarded.

Within Mahayana, there are still points to be cultivated and other to be abandoned, but above all, what matters most on this path of wisdom and love, is to attain a state of deep conviction about what phenomena really are.

At the relative level, phenomena exist in dependence upon causes and conditions. At the absolute level, phenomena exist according to a principle based on an uncreated, absolute dimension. Entering into the path of Bodhisattvas means having a thorough and deep understanding of relative and absolute truths.

Two truths

These words by Nagarjuna perfectly illustrate our subject: « Considering the whole Buddha's teaching, it can be summarized in its essence through this presentation of truths, the relative and the absolute ones ».

While traditionally studying scriptures, as it is currently done in monasteries or in shards (Buddhist universities), the two truths are differently presented according to the various philosophical schools of Hiragana and Mahayana.

Hinayana schools:

1. The Vaibhasika school is related to Shravakas.
2. The Sautrantika school, "the school of those who are following the Sutras".

Mahayana schools:

3. The Cittamatra school, "Mind only" also called "Yogacharya".
4. The Madhyamika school.

Relative truth, the expression of consciousness within misunderstanding

All possible manifested phenomena arising from the living worlds including all living creatures, human beings, animals, insects, visible and invisible beings, as well as phenomena belonging to the inanimate worlds, all phenomena from matter up to the omniscience of a Buddha, all of them do exist in dependence upon causes and conditions. These phenomena are perceived by ordinary people as quite natural and obvious, as being the reality, the true reality as it is depicted in the West, though there has been no further investigation about it. But how can it exist? The following truth seems to be quite obvious: « Once the seed has been sown, the sprout arises ». At this level, it is about relative truth or dissembling truth since it hides the absolute truth.

While analyzing the definition of relative truth which is available in different books, we can find that this relative truth refers to a consciousness that is mistaken, whose perceptions are distorted. It is designated as dissembling because this distorted perception is concealing the essence or true nature of the perceived phenomena. The point is not in perceiving phenomena, but in perceiving that these phenomena are a manifestation of emptiness.

Absolute truth, expression of emptiness

On one hand, we distinguish between ordinary mind, that is to say the mental and its distorted perceptions, and on the other hand wisdom. Wisdom arises through acknowledging emptiness, the absolute truth. The absolute truth refers to the uncreated dimension which is emptiness. Absolute truth (Skt. Loledepa, Tib. Marsamjodme) is transcending the intellect and is ineffable. "Marsamjodme" means that «Even if we wished to talk about it, it would not be possible». This reality, which is transcending the intellect, is the absolute truth. All possible manifesting phenomena are entailed in both truths. All phenomena are concerned by one of these two truths.

Presenting relative and absolute truth is a huge task, but these few definitions enable us to outline the topic.

The relative truth is perceived by a consciousness which functions in a dualistic way and which is spoiled because it is covered with veils. Absolute truth is perceived by a consciousness which does not work anymore according to a dualistic object/subject pattern. Perceptions occur through a non-dualistic mode and are totally pure.

2. View (Tib. Tava)

The view during the meditation stage

Understanding and realizing the non-self of persons occurs in a perfect way. During the meditation stage, this perfect view consists of understanding that in an absolute manner all phenomena are totally deprived of self-existence.

Only one reality prevails, which is as vast as uncreated space. In Tibetan, it refers to "tchötchen", which means a total absence of unfolding mental activity which is always interpreting, gossiping or rambling. When we are in this pure presence-awareness, connected to that kind of absolute dimension similar to infinite space, we are fully immersed in a state of great simplicity, whereby the mental does not have to produce, create or invent anything, there is a total lack of unfolding mental activity. Hence, there is a crystal-clear perception of a state called «Great Emptiness» in Sutras.

The view during the post-meditation stage

When we have completed the meditation stage, where we were immersed in this kind of space-like vast presence, and when we enter into the next stage, back to deal with our current daily matters and activities, we should hold and maintain the same view we had during the meditation stage and keep it flowing like a river stream. We can perceive, without any confusion, all phenomena in their finest details while perfectly being aware that they are not self-existing. We are able to properly keep on functioning in the relative world, respecting the social conventions, while knowing at the same time that it is all merely a kind of unfolding succession of appearances. The practitioner is able to live the so-called relative reality in respect to the eight metaphors of illusion: dream, echo, ghost, mirage, etc. (cf. page 33). We do not focus on a self-existence « from our own side» as they say in Tibetan. When we gaze at the night's sky, there is an immense space full of stars. We can have a total correct perception of the relative reality — that means seeing each star, one after the other very clearly and distinctly — while being connected to the absolute reality compared to sky. This is what is called proper view in respect to absolute, as well as relative reality.

What does the expression « attaining the view of emptiness » mean? It can not happen through a dualistic pattern since it is a global experience. The usual concept of a subject, inside, and of an object, outside, is somehow transcended, by a kind of alchemical process, into the innermost essence of emptiness. The concept of a subject which is "I" and of a world perceived by this subject is totally erased. Nothing is abandoned but everything is transmuted. What we have been experiencing up to now has always been referred to as subject and object and considered as a true reality, though it is basically just an illusion. The concept of subject/object will melt and become the very essence of emptiness.

It is fundamental to acknowledge this dimension referred to as emptiness. How? In the Madhyamakavatara, "Introduction to the middle path" translated by Louis de la Vallée-Poussin, Candrakirti, the author of this text, is presenting a way to realize emptiness.

Emptiness according to the Madhyamakavatara by Candrakirti

Prove by reasoning

There are seven types of great reasoning. Great reasoning helps us to cut through the blind belief we have regarding the self-existence of persons and phenomena. Through an argumentation, which may sometimes sound absurd, it leads us to the conclusion that our belief is groundless. The different reasonings, which are specific to the Madhyamika school lead us to a certainty: all tangible and non-tangible phenomena, up to the fully awakened mind of a Buddha, also called omniscience, prove how absurd our beliefs and representations are.

We gain the certainty that none of the tangible or non-tangible phenomena are self-existing. But this conviction remains at an intellectual level. We are limited to a mental representation which is certainly matching the reality, but is still based on an intellectual understanding.

Prove through meditation

Meditation enables us to consider emptiness as an awareness support. It means that the mind itself is realizing emptiness. If there is a consciousness realizing emptiness, it proves that there is actually no realization of emptiness. When we come to true contemplation, the concept of a subject who had intellectually understood emptiness is gradually disappearing. The Madhyamikavatara pinpoints that we can talk about proper way of realizing emptiness only when there is just a global experience of emptiness. There is no one realizing emptiness, there is only the core being of this reality.

As far as terminology related to the Sutras within Mahayana is concerned, the word "emptiness" (Skt. Shunyata, Tib. Tong-pa-nyid) is generally used, whereas in Dzogchen, we use Primordial Purity (Tib. Kadag). The methods proposed by Candrakirti from India, the country of Aryas, to gain full realization of Pristine Purity, and by Rongzom Mahapandita, a great Tibetan master of the 11th century, are alike.

For beginners, who have not yet the abilities to realize emptiness straight away, merely hearing these words, which can be found in many scriptures, stating that all phenomena look like a reflection in a mirror, an echo, a scarecrow taken for someone alive, a pile of stones taken for a human body, a dream, a mirage, a cloud, brings them closer to the realization of emptiness. Merely feeling and acknowledging that our whole being, at body, speech and mind level, as well as the entire world and all manifested appearances can not be grasped and are dream-like, brings us closer to the realization of emptiness, called Primordial Purity in Dzogchen.

3. Ethic (Tib. Tsültrim)

There are three types of ethic for Bodhisattvas.

a) Refraining from any kind of reprehensible behaviour.

b) Gathering as much positive and virtuous things as possible.

c) Acting in such a manner to benefit all beings.

a) Refraining from any kind of reprehensible behaviour

A vow (Skt. Samvara, Tib. Dompa) means "to knot", "to bind".

It is about controlling ourselves in order to avoid any kind of reprehensible action.

In Cittamatra, the school of "Mind only", there are twelve root misdeeds which make us sink and break our bodhisattva commitment.

Twelve root misdeeds of Bodhisattvas according to Cittamatra

1. Four white dharmas;

2. Four black dharmas;

3. Four root defects, which make us sink, partially or totally lose our Bodhisattva vows.

We are not going to detail these misdeeds.

According to the schools of Madhyamika, Svatantrikas and Prasangikas, Bodhisattvas strive not to commit twenty root misdeeds which break their Bodhisattva commitment.

Twenty Bodhisattva root misdeeds according to Madhyamika

1. Five misdeeds linked to being near a king.
2. Five misdeeds linked to being near a minister.
3. Eight misdeeds related to Hinayana.
4. Two misdeeds related to aspiration and application Bodhicittas.

1. Five misdeeds linked to being near a king

a) Stealing goods and offerings made to the Three Jewels.

b) Giving up Dharma.

c) Making people break their commitment.

For example, convincing a monk not to take the bhiksu vows.

d) Carrying out one of the five deeds causing immediate retribution: killing one's father, killing one's mother, killing an Arhat, hurting a Buddha or making him bleed with a bad intention, making the sangha split apart. The result of any of these deeds is falling down into hell without going through the intermediate stage of bardo.

e) Developing distorted views.

Because of his power, a king can steal offerings made to the Three Jewels, forbid people of his realm to take vows, or seized by a burst of rage he may carry out highly reprehensible deeds or give up Dharma, and so forth... Like powerful kings, Bodhisattvas must pay attention not to carry out any of these misdeeds, which might nevertheless occur so easily.

2. Five misdeeds linked to being near a minister

a) Destroying a hamlet.

b) Destroying a village.

c) Destroying a town.

d) Destroying a capitale city.

e) Destroying a country.

3. Eight misdeeds related to Hinayana:

a) Presenting emptiness to someone who may be disturbed by it.

b) Turning a Bodhisattva off the path of Mahayana, making him or her enter a lower path by telling him or her for instance that the hearers' path is better.

c) Being a bad guide for someone who has taken Bodhisattva vows and pushing him or her to break them in order to take vows of individual liberation (Skt. Pratimoksha).

d) Being a bad guide for someone who has taken Pratimoksha vows, and driving him or her to take bodhisattva vows by telling that his or her path is a lower one. Prompting someone to break his or her Pratimoksha vows.

e) Denigrating the hearer's path by pretending that it does not enable to realize full Enlightenment. This truth should not be the opportunity to denigrate the Shravakas' path.

f) Criticizing others because of jealousy, and praising oneself.

g) Misleading a lama by denigrating one of his disciples so that the concerned disciple will be blamed.

h) Making hindrances to people engaged in meditation so that they will not be able to reach their goal.

4. Two misdeeds related to Bodhicittas

- **To aspiration's Bodhicitta:** Completely abandoning beings and following our ego-centred matters.

- **To application's Bodhicitta:** Being truly involved by deeds in an approach opposed to aspiration vows and giving them up definitely.

We are coming back now to the second point related to the ethic of a Bodhisattva.

b) Gathering as much positive and virtuous things as possible.

It consists of practicing the six Paramitas (perfections). We will develop them later on when we will study the Bodhisattva behaviour (cf. page 71).

c) Acting in such a manner to benefit all beings.

To accomplish this third point of the ethic, it is necessary for the Bodhisattva to gather disciples.

There are four ways to gather disciples:

1. Practising generosity, attracting people through generosity.

2. Talking with a smooth voice to create friendly relationships.

3. Adapting oneself to the different people we are talking to.

4. Prompting people to enter the Bodhisattvas' path.

4. Meditation. (Tib. Gompa)

Meditation deals with the thirty-seven points to Enlightenment divided into four paths (Tib. Lam). The first four paths are called "learning paths". The fifth path is a non-learning path as it corresponds to the Bhumi of Full Enlightenment, namely fruition.

The four learning's paths are:

a) The preparation's path
b) The implementation's path
c) The vision's path
d) The meditation's path

The thirty-seven points to Enlightenment

They unfold and develop as we move along these four paths.

1. The four "skills" to stabilizing attention
2. The four perfect giving ups
3. The four grounds
4. The five abilities
5. The five powers
6. The seven branches of Enlightenment
7. The eight branches of the path

a) The preparation's path

Tibetan people prefer to call it "accumulation's path". It is somehow like making, namely accumulating all kinds of preparations in the perspective of a journey.

On the preparation path, there are three levels: **a.1)** the small preparation path, **a.2)** the intermediate preparation path and **a.3)** the great preparation path.

a.1) The small preparation path:

Here we have to cultivate the four ways of stabilizing sustained attention, in respect to body, perceptions, mind and phenomena.

The four "skills" to stabilizing attention

1. Stabilizing attention in respect to body:

During a meditation session, the body is regarded as emptiness, and while doing our daily activities, it is regarded as an illusion. During the post-meditation stage, the body is seen as spoiled, mortal, perishable an even liable to putrefaction. It is even possible to remind us that the body is doomed to end in a cemetery or as a corpse in a charnel-grave as it was usual in ancient India. This meditation counterbalances any kind of attachment to the body. We can meditate this way on the body or in a more gentle way, for example meditating the body in respect to the eight metaphors of illusion, namely as a dream, a mirage, a moon reflection into water, and so forth...

2. Stabilizing attention in respect to perceptions:

This skill consists of tightly stabilizing attention in respect to perceptions which may be experienced as suffering, happiness or neutral. Within the meditation stage, the point is to contemplate all kinds of perceptions as being emptiness. Within the post-meditation stage, the aim is to consider all kinds of perceptions, pleasant, unpleasant or neutral ones, as being impermanent, and thus being deprived of any self-essence.

3. Stabilizing attention in respect to mind:

This skill aims at stabilizing the mind (Tib. Sem), understood here in a very open way. In Tibetan "Sem" is related to a capacity to experience, to being aware.

Within the meditation stage, the point is to consider the mind, namely our inner capacity of awareness, as being the absolute reality, namely Dharmata.

Within the post-meditation stage, the point is to recognize the mind as being part of the union essence of luminous clarity and emptiness. Clarity corresponds to the ability of being fully aware. This ability is endowed with a radiant luminous clarity and at the same time it is space-like uncreated, thus it is empty.

4. Stabilizing attention in respect to phenomena:

Here the skill consists of stabilizing attention in respect to phenomena (Skt. Dharma).

During the meditation phase, phenomena are experienced as empty, deprived from any self or intrinsic existence. It is an experience related to wholeness, referring to the uncreated reality. During the post-meditation phase, phenomena are experienced in accordance with the eight metaphors of illusion, since phenomena merely exist upon causes and conditions or karma law. When causes and conditions are gathered, phenomena arise and then disappear.

a.2) The intermediate preparation's path:

Once they are on the intermediate preparation path, Bodhisattvas strive to uphold the four perfect giving ups:

The four perfect giving ups

1. The first perfect giving up:

Bodhisattvas never produce any negative energy. May it happen that a negative element arises in their mind, they let it go immediately.

2. The second perfect giving up:

Bodhisattvas focus their efforts in making all positive dharmas, namely all positive energy within them, but not born yet, appear. They give up all hindrances which prevent this positive energy to be produced and manifested.

3. The third perfect giving up:

They give up the fact of not being attached to have this positive energy arise.

4. The fourth perfect giving up:

Once positive energy is generated, Bodhisattvas take care to have it grow more and more. They refrain themselves from being careless about its growing and developing.

a.3) The great preparation's path:

On the great preparation path, there are "four grounds", namely powers (Skt. siddhis) related to the four meditative absorptions.

The four grounds

1. The first ground: aspiration's power.

2. The second ground: power of energy put into practice.

3. The third ground: power of thinking.

4. The fourth ground: action's power.

We talk about four grounds to show that Bodhisattvas have to unfold and develop a great moral energy and inner strength in order to be able to cross the preparation's path, which leads to the implementation's path.

b) The implementation's path

The implementation's path deals with five learning abilities.

The five abilities

1. Trust/faith;

2. Energy and enthusiastic perseverance;

3. Sustained attention, ability not to forget;

4. Concentration;

5. Awakened awareness (Tib. Sherab) that will become wisdom (Tib. Yeshe).

When it comes to implement these five abilities, there are two distinct stages: the warming up and the peak stages. All depends on the intensity and the level of perfecting of these five abilities.

When Bodhisattvas are still in the learning stage, it corresponds to an average intensity power, thus it is called «warming up stage». When these five abilities have gained their highest power, it is called «peak stage». A sustained training is needed in order to invigorate and enhance these five abilities. Hence, they will enable Bodhisattvas to reach out the peak of the implementation's path.

The five strengths

It refers to the five previously mentioned abilities

developed at their highest degree of intensity. They have become true strengths against any impediment.

These first two paths of Bodhisattvas, the preparation and implementation ones are meant for ordinary people, not that Bodhisattvas are ordinary people, but at this stage, as they do not have direct view of the absolute yet, they are still ordinary Bodhisattvas. Therefore, they are not noble beings yet, not yet Aryabodhisattvas.

c) The vision's path

The vision's path deals with the seven branches to Enlightenment:

The seven branches to Enlightenment

1. Attention.
2. Awakened awareness allowing discernment.
3. Enthusiasm, energy and perseverance.
4. Joy.
5. Flexibility.
6. Concentration.
7. Equanimity.

Engaged on the vision's path, Bodhisattvas have become superior beings (Skt. Arya, Tib. Phag-pa). They are now in the direct view of the absolute. At a coarse level, the thirty-seven factors of Enlightenment are not tainted any longer by the energy of yearning and aggression. Yet the subtle level remains tainted by it.

d) The meditation's path

The meditation's path deals with the eight branches of the Aryabodhisattva path:

The eight branches of the Aryabodhisattva path

1. The perfect view;
2. The perfect realization;
3. The perfect word;
4. The perfect karma field;

5. The perfect means of living;
6. The perfect efforts;
7. The perfect attention;
8. The perfect concentration.

Now you have a clear presentation of the thirty-seven factors of Enlightenment taking place on the four learning's paths of Bodhisattvas. Now you know how a Bodhisattva journey looks like.

5. Conduct (Tib. Chop)

The six Paramitas enfolds the very heart of the Bodhisattva training on the Mahayana's path.

The six Paramitas

1. Generosity, a capacity to give easily;
2. Ethic, a capacity to uphold vows and commitments;
3. Patience, a capacity to give up any thought of anger;
4. Enthusiastic perseverance or diligence, a kind of energy driven by deep joy;
5. Concentration, a capacity to calm abiding;
6. Wisdom or awakened awareness, a capacity to discriminate.

Each of these perfections can entail six divisions.

For example generosity:
1. Generosity-Generosity;
2. Ethic-Generosity;
3. Patience-Generosity;
4. Perseverance-Generosity;
5. Concentration-Generosity;
6. Wisdom-Generosity.

And so forth for each of the five others Paramitas.

As a result there are thirty-six ways of practicing Paramitas for Bodhisattvas. Bodhisattva's practices are infinite, that is why they are so often compared to the immensity of the ocean.

6. Result (Tib. Drebu)

When Bodhisattvas have achieved all different practices of the paramitas, they have attained the eleventh bhumi which is called Total Light: this is the level of a Buddha, the bhumi of Spreading Light. Fruition refers here to the fifth path, the path of no more learning for it is the bhumi of Full Enlightenment.

Kriya tantra, the path of ritual action

Feelings of renouncement and non-self

On the path of hearers and "self-Buddhas", the meditation phase takes us into the heart of the absolute dimension. But this meditative moment has to be embraced by understanding and knowledge which will lead to realizing the non-self.

The whole spiritual life of a practitioner is built upon two linking phases: «meditative equipoise posture» during the meditation session itself, and the « post-meditation stage» referring to the intersession time. Even if the intersession time is prevailing for lay people who work, the entire daily life should be considered as a support for meditation.

In the interval stage, it is necessary that a sense of renouncement embrace everything we are experiencing.

On the path of Mahayana, when Bodhisattvas are placed in meditative equipoise, they are overwhelmed by this understanding of non-self, which becomes realization, a state of mind «totally deprived from any mental unfolding activity».

The eight extremes views and the four immeasurables

As soon as the concept of "I" is present, the mental is stimulated and starts interpreting and judging. During the meditation stage, Bodhisattvas, who are at first un-directly, then directly connected with the absolute reality, are absorbed in this state, whereby there is no mental unfolding and the following eight extremes or negations are strayed away (Skt. Astanta, Tib. Tha-gyad): generation, cessation, nihilism, eternalism, comings and goings process, identity, diversity. This is clearly explained in the Madhyamika scriptures.

When Bodhisattvas enter into the post-meditation stage and go back to their daily activities, they should pay attention not to be parted from the four immeasurables which are love, joy, compassion and equanimity. These four immeasurables are nurturing Bodhicitta, the Heart of Enlightenment. Bodhisattvas are never parted from these four thoughts, thus, it enables great love and compassion to gradually develop and mature within Bodhicitta. As they are fully permeated by these four immeasurables, their actions and deeds are meant to serve and benefit beings.

Three purities

On the path of secret mantras, namely tantrayana or Vajrayana, which is also called vehicle of Vidyadharas, practitioners do perceive in the meditation stage that this vast reality is totally resulting from the uncreated dimension. When entering then the post-meditation stage, they are impregnated by three aspects of purity.

1. The first purity means that all visual perceptions of the practitioner are linked to the guru's or deity's body, the body of the practised yidam.

2. The second purity means that all auditory perceptions of the practitioner are like the guru's or the practised deity's words, namely the corresponding mantra of the practice.

3. The third purity means that every thought of the practitioner is experienced as belonging to the dharmakaya that is to say to the wisdom mind of the guru and of the deity. These thoughts are merely experienced as an unfolding, an activity or a distraction of the dharmakaya, the perfectly awakened mind.

The tantric practitioners, and this is what makes their path so special, are completely rooted in this vision of infinite purity.

Integration process of the three vehicles

The integration process of the three great Yana involves that none of the foundations of any of these three vehicles should be put aside or forgotten when we shift from a lower to an upper vehicle. Starting on the Bodhisattvas' path, the concept of renouncement peculiar to Hinayana, is not abandoned, but instead fully integrated within the path. While entering Vajrayana, the concept of love and compassion, which is inherent to Mahayana, is totally nurturing the tantras practitioners. Looking with despise at the foundations of the so-called "lower" vehicles is completely wrong. The instructions of the different vehicles build a full corpus which should be integrated by practitioners in its wholeness. The qualities or characteristic features of the first vehicle should be taken into the following vehicle. Every aspect of the first vehicle that makes it so special — the sense of renouncement and above all the experience of the non-self of persons — must be carefully kept when practitioners step into Mahayana. They keep within themselves what they have achieved and gained and open up to all the living creatures. They develop loving and compassion connections, which enable them to fully experience the wonderful adventure of a Bodhisattva.

When practitioners enter into Vajrayana, this treasure is in their heart. Renouncement, non-self of persons, non-self of phenomena and emptiness of all phenomena are their working ground which will enable them to open up to the radiant, bright and pure unfolding of the uncreated space.

The three baskets are the foundation stone of all the Buddha's teachings.

1. The Vinayapitaka discards the energy of desire and attachment;

2. The Sutrapitaka uproots the energy of anger and aggression;

3. The Abhidharmapitaka deletes the energy of ignorance.

These three baskets make a whole set of instructions. Practitioners should have a complete picture of these instructions and not a sketchy one. The practice should not be fragmentary. Instead of separating the baskets, we should rather integrate the three together in a global approach. By this way, it will be easy to attain Enlightenment.

Reminder

The nine Yana can be classified into three sets:

1. "The rising vehicle through emanation" enables beings to get out of the six realms of existence, to be freed from Kleshas and contaminated karma which are the driving force of Samsara. This encompasses the vehicles of Shravakas, Pratyekabuddhas and Bodhisattvas.

2. "The vehicle of knowledge through asceticism", namely the vehicle of outer tantras. It entails vehicles of Kriya, Charya and Yoga tantras.

3. "The vehicle of transcending skilful means", namely the vehicle of inner tantras. It embraces the vehicle of Maha, Anu and Ati yoga.

The three outer Tantras correspond to the vehicle leading to knowledge through asceticism. It is firstly necessary to distinguish between outer and inner Tantras. Why is there a distinction between inner and outer Tantras within the Vajrayana tradition?

Differences between outer and inner Tantras

1. The first explanation about outer Tantras refers to the usual practising method which deals much more with body and speech than with mind, as it will be the case with inner Tantras. Merely having a good body and life hygiene and controlling speech by using pleasant and kind words will enable to reach out the expected goal and recognize Rigpa, the awakened knowledge.

2. The second explanation is based on the fact that the practitioner is not capable yet to put into practice all the instructions concerning the four empowerments of the inner Tantras. These four empowerments are: the vase empowerment, the secret empowerment, the supreme wisdom empowerment and the precious speech empowerment.

Here practitioners remain at the level of the first empowerment, the vase empowerment as they are not ready yet to begin the practices related to the three following empowerments, which are gradually higher and higher.

Differences between Sutras and Tantras

It is necessary to distinguish between Sutras (Tib. Do) and Tantras (Tib. Gyu). Tantras are superior to Sutras through four aspects: view, practice, gained result and disciple.

A word from a Tantra says: « The final sought aim in Sutras and Tantras is the same». The final aim sought by Bodhisattvas is full Enlightenment. At the Sutras level, the self-existing wisdom/knowledge (Tib. Rigpa) which is the main point in Vajrayana, is somehow covered by veils and defilements. Here it is still a lot about ordinary consciousness stained by the mental (Tib. SEM)

The four reasons that make Vajrayana a superior path

1. Vajrayana is regarded as a higher path because wisdom is being unveiled or uncovered. A distinction is made between «what is clouded» and « what is not clouded ». Within Sutrayana, Rigpa, this primordial wisdom/knowledge is still covered or veiled, whereas in Vajrayana, Rigpa is being uncovered.

2. Unlike Sutrayana, Vajrayana offers a great choice of skillful means, specific to Vajrayana, which consist of different techniques and methods to achieve pure vision. These skilful means enable our Buddha nature to arise. As a result, our innermost essence, which had been hidden up to this very moment, can manifest and be used to rise ourselves to the level of pure vision.

3. In Vajrayana it is quite easy to apply the offered skilful means, which enable practitioners to progress swiftly or even amazingly on the path, without going through strict asceticism. These means allow to move forward on the path rather with comfort and easiness. It is possible within one lifetime to completely eliminate even the finest veils and hence to reveal in its pure nakedness primordial Enlightenment that had remained hidden.

Vajrayana is characterized by a lack of difficulties and certain quickness, whereas Sutrayana can last over lifetimes and lifetimes. As a matter of fact, "He, who manifested full Enlightenment in Bodhgaya", in India, had to spend three great kalpas to cleanse the veils from his mind. Through this accumulation of immeasurable merits, the Bodhisattva was able to offer his own body to a hungry tigress. The lightning power of this self-offering made him reborn in Tushita before he became the fourth Buddha in our kalpa. Within Vajrayana, thanks to the union of wisdom and skilful means, it is possible to be in one and the same time enjoying ourselves even by drinking alcohol, eating meat or having sex. Thanks to the union of skilful means and awakened awareness, it is possible to transcend and integrate every thing at a sensory level and thus, make this firewood increase the wisdom fire in order to reach Enlightenment within one lifetime.

Within Hinayana or within Theravada, Southern Buddhism, a monk coming from countries like Skri Lanka, Burma, Thailand, Laos, Cambodia or Vietnam, is forbidden to receive money, gold, precious metals or stones, to take alcohol or to eat meat. Even if it may sometimes happen to meet monks eating meat, there are still many interdicts.

Within Vajrayana — we can see it during tsok offering — meat and alcohol are samaya substances. It is usual to add a little bit of alcohol and meat in the tsok offering, which we can take with pure vision. During such an offering these substances are transmuted into elements filled with special wisdom energy. In respect to tantric practices, it is possible that the practitioner is not chaste and has got a partner or a consort.

The tantric consort

It is often said that all Nyingmapa masters have a consort. It is not the case, but however it is true that in Tibet there was sometimes this kind of incisive judgement, that all Nyingmapas were alcoholised and corrupted. Nevertheless, if we are a genuine tantric practitioner, it is useful to think deeply about it and ask our guru to know if we have got the capacity to have a tantric partner, since it is a very serious matter. If we assume to have this capacity and if our guru agrees, then this loving and sensorial experience will benefit us. It will enable us to progress on the path, to increase wisdom. But if we are not yet ready for this kind of experience, it can cause lots of problems.

4. The fourth reason that makes Vajrayana superior to Sutrayana refers to the four qualities endowed by tantric practitioners.

The four qualities of disciples

a) The first quality is a great sharpness of mind and great insight ability.

b) The second quality conveys that this smartness is filled with trust, faith, admiration and appreciation. Disciples in their connection to the guru, to the deity and to the world are endowed with pure vision, freshness and purity.

c) The third quality of tantric practitioners is their ability to perfectly and purely uphold the five root samayas which are binding them to their master. This is a crucial point.

d) The fourth quality referring to and justifying the expression of "sharp faculties" — which has nothing to do with intelligence — consists of their capacity of developing pure vision. This is the foundation of Vajrayana. Disciples must be able to understand that the guru, during empowerment, is introducing them to this dimension of infinite purity. The principle of the "three purities" (cf. page 74) implies that all visual and auditory perceptions are regarded as the body of the guru or the deity, the words of the guru or the deity ; thoughts are regarded as a mere unfolding of Dharmakaya, a distraction of the fully awakened mind.

We have already seen that Mahayana is more imposing than Hinayana. It would be a little bit like comparing an eagle with a small bird. Similarly Vajrayana, the vehicle of Tantras, is superior to Sutrayana because of the four specificities we have just mentioned.

In the first verse of the Heruka Karpo Tantra of the ancient school, it is said that within Sutrayana, the proper nature of consciousness, which is related to the nature of Clear Light, is shown as being the cause of Enlightenment. This is the reason why it is referred to "causal vehicle of characteristic features". In the second verse of the Heruka Karpo Tantra, it is said that whithin Vajrayana, "the vehicle of secret mantras", we should meditate on the proper nature of mind as being an awakened mind.

In the first case, the proper nature of mind is regarded as being the cause of Enlightenment. In the second case, the proper nature of mind is Enlightenment, Buddhahood itself.

Introduction to the nature of mind

When we reach out the peak level of Vajrayana, namely Dzogchen, we first of all have to be introduced to Rigpa, the nature of mind. Not only can the master introduce the disciple to the nature of mind. Once disciples have completed special practices, they can recognize the nature of their mind by themselves and sometimes even in a very swift and impressive manner.

How does this introduction to Rigpa conferred by the guru to the disciple occur?

In a very fleeting moment, the guru makes the disciple be aware that Enlightenment is precisely here, that the infinite and luminous space-like nature of mind, namely Dharmakaya, has always been here. Prayers from different traditions, including the Kagyü one, express then praises to the master: « Ô guru, you have allowed me to recognize the nature of my mind as being the Dharmakaya ». There are instructions directly conferred by the guru to the disciples for practices, empowerments and precepts. They are fast, efficient and powerful methods specific to Vajrayana. Once his disciples have accomplished a certain preparation work, the guru makes them aware of this reality, which has always been here. Sometimes there is a strong heart or even karmic connection between the guru and his disciples.

Disciples can then catch a brief glimpse of the great Enlightenment or Dharmakaya, as this precept expresses it very well: « Meditate the very nature of mind as being Enlightenment itself ». This is the reason why fruition is linked to the secret mantras vehicle since disciples are made aware of this pristine reality that is fruition. Fruition merely consists of assessing what has been primordially present.

Kriya Tantra, the Tantra of ritual action

Kriya Tantra is the first of the three outer Tantras which build with the Charya and Yoga Tantras, "the knowledge vehicle through asceticism".

What are the characteristic features of the Kriya Tantra? The view is completely freed of the "four extremes", namely the existence, the non-existence, both of them and none of them. This absolute is beyond the conceptual classifications of what is existing or not.

In the meditation stage, at the absolute level, practitioners remain in this view that is beyond all kinds of extremes.

In the post-meditation stage, at the relative level, practitioners create a connection with their yidam, whom they somehow regard as being their superior or their boss.

The yidam is still a support for hope. We expect from the yidam all signs of success and accomplishments (Skt. Siddhi, Tib. Dngö Drub). We imagine that the deity is like the supreme authority, who would grant awards if we have been good yogis or yoginis.

What is the specificity of Kriya Tantra? Kriya means "making or doing", "activity". Why is it about activity or action Tantras? Because the required efforts are specifically related to body and speech, whereas in higher Tantras, also called unsurpassable Tantras, efforts are rather related to mind, which has to become subtler and purer.

Kriya Tantra, like other vehicles, contains six great linking points.

The six linking points

1. Entrance's door (Tib. Jugo)

Kriya Tantra entails a unique characteristic feature since there are two gateways.

a) The first door of entrance

The first entrance's door consists of five empowerments.

The five empowerments:

1. Water empowerment.
2. Crown empowerment.
3. Empowerment of the Vajra disciple.
4. Protection empowerment.
5. Empowerment of the eight auspicious substances.

1. Water empowerment

The aim of the water empowerment is to fertilize the seed of the Dharmakaya realization or fully awakened mind. When the guru is conferring the water empowerment, he is fertilizing in the disciple mind the seeds, which will mature and bring the fruits of Dharmakaya, namely the awakened mind.

2. Crown empowerment

When the guru is conferring the crown empowerment, also called silk cap empowerment, the guru is fertilizing in the disciple mind the seeds, which will mature in the two kinds of kayas: the Sambhogakaya, which is the first subtlest manifestation body and the Nirmanakaya, which can be a human or animal incarnation to serve beings. These first two empowerments of water and crown are the two true main empowerments of the activity Tantras.

3. Empowerment of the vajra disciple

During the empowerment of the vajra disciple, the vajra master (Tib. Dordje Lopön) symbolically displays the mandala on which the disciple throws a flower. The place reached by the flower at one of the four cardinal points or in the centre of the mandala, shows to which family of the five dhyanis Buddhas the disciple belongs for the present empowerment. The vajra master explains to his disciple to which family he belongs: the centre refers to Vairocana, the east to Akshobya, the south to Ratnasambhava, the west to Amitabha and the north to Amoghasiddhi.

4. Protection empowerment

The protection empowerment has two functions. The first one is to protect the vajra disciple, who is entering into the mandala, within the circle of a dhyani Buddha. The aim is to chase the hindrances makers, who might impede the vajra disciple in his practices. The second function of this empowerment is also to bath the disciple, to cleanse and to protect him.

5. The empowerment of the eight auspicious substances

The aim of the empowerment of the eight auspicious substances is to increase all favourable conditions within the disciple life so that he can practice easily and diligently.

b) The second entrance's door

The second entrance's door consists of three purities, three baths and three cleanlinesses.

The three purities

1. The first aspect regards the deity and the mandalas.

2. The second aspect deals with refraining oneself from taking meat, fish, eggs, onions and even garlic. The practitioner pays attention to keep his kitchen perfectly neat and tidy, and use perfectly clean cooking and kitchen utensils.

3. The third aspect refers to mantra and concentration. Whatever mantra the disciple practices after the conferred empowerment, the repetition of this mantra will lead the practitioner to a kind of natural samadhi.

The three aspects of purity consist of developing an inner purity, which, through the mantra repetition and the deity contemplation will cleanse Kleshas, and an outer purity through avoiding eating meat, which is against life.

The three baths

The word "bath" has to be understood in regard to the context of ancient India, where it was important to have a strict body hygiene, but also to live in a neat and tidy environment and wear clean clothes.

The three baths are experienced at three levels: outer, inner and secret ones.

1. Outer bath consists of washing what Tibetan call the five limbs, namely two arms, two legs and the trunk.

2. Inner bath consists of purifying the subtle channels (Tib. Tsa) and inner winds (Tib. Lung).

3. The secret bath consists of cleansing all factors opposed to the view and resulting from the dualistic grasping, which implies the concept of subject and object and at a subtler level working with marks and signs. We think there is an outer objective reality with its own characteristic features. This kind of belief as well as thoughts are impediments and opposed to the right view. The bath consists of cleansing ourselves from our ordinary mental and from the dualistic view, which is usually related to it. By this way, we manage to rise ourselves to the level of the perfect view (Tib. Tava).

The three cleanlinesses

The three cleanlinesses deal with the clothes worn at outer, inner and secret levels.

1. Outer cleanliness refers to wearing clean clothes.

2. Inner cleanliness involves properly upholding vows.

3. Secret cleanliness consists of meditating the deity.

First we receive the five empowerments, then we strive ourselves to put into practice the three purities, baths and cleannessess. For example, if we are engaged in an intensive practice of the venerable Tara, that is the most familiar and known deity of the Kriya Tantras, it is important to refrain ourselves from taking meat, fish, onions and so forth. Hence, we can create a pure space, which enables us to be linked to the deity.

2. View (Tib. Tava)

At the absolute level, the practitioner understands that his own mind has in essence no foundation. The mind is far from being any kind of entity. Can one ever tell what mind is! The practitioner understands that his or her own consciousness is primordially unborn and groundless. Mind, in the noble meaning of the word, that is to say beyond the mental layers, has nothing to do with thoughts. The practitioner discovers that mind belongs to the uncreated dimension and therefore is beyond any kind of discursive unfolding.

The non-existence of good and bad

The non-existence of good and bad is the keystone of Kriya Tantras. The practitioner understands that these notions of good and bad at the absolute level have indeed no foundation. Furthermore, at a relative level, he or she is not in a dualistic state of mind. However, the practitioner considers the yidam as being superior, more extraordinary and praiseworthy. The practitioner involved in practices, for example practising the noble Tara, is filled with this kind of trust, faith and devotion. He or she is serving the deity, praising her, making offerings and chanting but in one and the same time hoping to receive in return her blessings and some siddhis. This practitioner is already endowed with a very high view, but nevertheless at a relative level, he or she is establishing with the practised deity a king-to-subject-like relationship, even if at the absolute level we know that everything is alike, that there is neither good nor bad.

The king-to-subject-like relationship with the deity

The relationship between the practitioner and the deity is one of a superior to his/her subordinate. The former one is able to confer blessings, allowing to achieve realizations, and the latter looks rather like a servant. Thanks to their devotion and faith, total trust and relying on the grace and generosity of the deity, practitioners can realize the deity.

Realizing the deity means being able to receive her grace and blessing, which will make us mature and allow her potential qualities to rise and develop.

Difference between Bodhisattva of Sutras and practitioner of the first Tantras

In the Tantras of the ritual action, Tantrikas do not consider their mind and the deity's mind as different. They regard the awakened mind of the deity as being superior to their own mind. They do not experience the inseparability of the yidam and their own mind, as it is the case in the upper Tantras. However, they develop the certainty that by doing so and following the guru's instructions, they will be able to realize the deity. Comparatively, the Bodhisattva, who follows the vehicle of Sutras can also understand at the absolute level that nothing is self-existing, that everything results from an uncreated essence. From this point of view, the Bodhisattva is not inferior to the Tantrika and has no cause to be jealous of him. Both of them understand that at a relative level, the whole reality is simply an illusion as referred to in the eight metaphors about dreamlike appearances.

So, what makes them different? Pure vision: here starts Vajrayana. This is what makes the difference between the Bodhisattva of Sutras and the practitioner of the first Tantras.

Thanks to the empowerment, practitioners discover the purity of Rigpa, that is to say the purity of the nature of mind. During their practice they realize that the mind is not an ordinary one: it is Rigpa, the purest and subtlest aspect of mind, the great awareness of the absolute. From this experience, practitioners get familiar with the purity of every perceived thing. The main difference with the Bodhisattva of Sutras is that the Tantrika perceives relative phenomena not only as illusions, but also as unfoldings of pure wisdom.

3. Ethic (Tib. Tsültrim)

Within Vajrayana, the ethic consists of upholding samayas. In Kriya Tantra, there are five root samayas and six secondary samayas, which make eleven samayas.

The five root samayas:

1. No sleeping in a high bed.
2. No eating meat, being vegetarian.
3. No taking alcohol.
4. No eating garlic.
5. No eating radishes.

In Asia, there are long white radishes. Eating radishes and garlic produces a kind of body pollution.

The six secondary samayas:

1. No abandoning the Three Jewels.
2. No abandoning Bodhicitta, the Heart of Enlightenment.
3. No abandoning the mantra and the deity or yidam.
4. Never being separated from the vajra and the bell,

symbols of skilful means and wisdom. We should always keep them by ourselves or have pictures of them, since they represent the samayas that are binding us to the five Victorious, namely the five dhyani Buddhas.

5. No abandoning the chosen deity that we practise.

6. No abandoning the guru or spiritual friend.

4. Meditation. (Tib. Gompa)

Meditation consists of four "being-as-it-is" in respect to the absolute dimension: « a state of the absolute that is just as it is ».

The four being-as-it-is

1. Being-as-it-is of the self.
2. Being-as-it-is of the deity with its six aspects.
3. Being-as-it-is of the mantra recitation.
4. Being-as-it-is of meditation.

1. Being-as-it-is of the self.

Being-as-it-is of the self consists of being earthed and grounded in the natural state of non-self. It is about experiencing this reality as being the "self", parted from all other things. This experience actually belongs to the absolute way of being of the base. Practitioners succeed in having the impure and stained notions of subject and object reabsorbed.

The subject-object relationship

From the moment up where there is a notion of self as subject, a stained and distorted view of the absolute reality automatically appears. As soon as the notion of subject arouses, the notion of object immediately appears, which in its turn will also be distorted and stained. When we can get out of this spoiled pattern of subject-object, then it is possible to connect to Yeshe, the wisdom dimension, of which we usually have no idea because of that "I" which pollutes the mental.

Freed from this distorting view of subject-object, we can

access to the notion of wisdom, and from that very point, we can connect to the deity. As long as we are stuck with the notion of "I" or "self", it is not possible to be linked to the deity. The being-as-it-is of self enables us to connect to the deity. When we can access to this wisdom dimension, thus we can access to the absolute deity. The deity upon whom we are focusing appears at a relative level, merely being an emanation. However, in respect to the absolute truth, it refers to wisdom dimension, to absolute Bodhicitta.

2. Being-as-it-is of the deity with its six aspects

Two practices of the Kriya Tantra:

a) The simple one.

b) The special one.

a) The simple practice

The simple practice of Kriya Tantra consists of the generation stage in front of us (Tib. Dun Kye). The deity is visualized in front of us. In Tibetan it is called « The clarity is cultivated ». We let the deity unfold in front of us in its clear dimension.

b) The special practice

The special practice of Kriya Tantra consists of the generation phase of ourselves (Tib. Dak Kye) as pure mind. Practitioners generate themselves as pure mind, under the features of the yidam.

All Tantras involve a "Dak Kye" practice; only in the higher Tantras is the generation of the deity immediate.

The six aspects of the «Dak Kye» specific to Kriya Tantra

b.1) Meditation of the void deity

At the absolute level, it is about meditating ourselves as a void deity. The aim is to be aware that the self takes part into the absolute uncreated dimension.

b.2) Meditation of the deity as a letter

At a relative level, we meditate a bright white moon disc, laid flat and used as a seat. The moon disc arises from a root-letter (Skt. Bija, Tib. Sa-bön), which originally results from a written form and a sound. This is the reason why the meditation upon the moon disc is called the deity of the letter or the sign.

b.3) Meditation of the deity related to sound

In the middle of the moon disc arises the root-letter of the deity. If we meditate the Venerable Tara, it is the green root-letter TAM. If we meditate Amitabha, it is a red HRI. On the moon disc, the root-letter in the middle is surrounded by a chain of the mantra letters to be recited according to the practised Yidam. This meditation, which enables to see clearly the root-syllable and the mantra, and thus to cultivate clarity is called meditation related to sound.

b.4) Meditation of the deity related to form

It is called the "meditation of the deity related to form" (Skt. Rüpa, Tib. Zug) since the deity appears with the form of a body. In a first time luminous rays radiate from the root-syllable and from the different mantra letters. In the upwards directions they honour all awakened beings and Buddhas with offerings. They prompt them to accomplish activities which enable sentient beings to be free of confusion. When this prayer is completed, the luminous rays melt into the central letter and the mantra letters at the periphery. The moon disc and the letters representing the essential repeated sound as mantra, as well as the rays that have come back loaded merge in one substance, which then turns into the body features of the practised deity.

For example, if we practise Manjushri, we visualize the root-syllable Dhi, which then turns into Manjushri appearing in a bright orange colour. When the deity appears in its full radiance, it is called the meditation of the deity related to form.

b.5) Meditation of the deity related to mudra

Let's first have a look at the different meanings of the word "mudra". Mudra (Tib. Tchag Gya) has many meanings. In respect to higher practices, mudra is the name given to the consort. Mudra also refers to the attributes held by the deity in her hands. Manjushri is visualized flourishing the wisdom sword and the prajna book. Four-armed Tchenrezi is visualized holding in his hands a white lotus, a crystal rosary (Tib. Mala) and the jewel (Tib. Norbu). Mudra means "sealed with attributes held by hands". In the example of Manjushri, the meditation of this deity related to form would not be complete, if it was deprived of the corresponding attributes. The meditation is somehow sealed by the visualization of the deity attributes: the sword and the prajna book.

b.6) Meditation of the deity related to signs and marks

With sustained concentration we meditate the deity as undifferentiated from ourselves. We make one with the deity, but at the same time, the deity still appears with her attributes and specific features. For example, Manjushri appears with his own features, orange-like colour, silky ornaments and attributes.

The special practice aims at generating oneself as the deity (Tib. Dak Kye). Within the meditation of the deity related to signs and marks in the context of Kriya Tantra, we can not really say that we are the deity, but simultaneously, we are involved in the nature of the deity.

3. Being-as-it-is of the mantra recitation

The being-as-it-is of the mantra recitation entails three parts:

a) "Rooting in the base" means that there is a perfect focusing on the deity visualized in front of us. We invest our entire attention power in accurately focusing on the deity. It is called rooting in the base. The deity is compared to a base in which our attention is sunk as an arrow in its target.

b) "Rooting in the mind" means meditating a moon disc, which is laid in the heart of the deity located in front of us. It is called rooting in the mind, focusing on the moon disc.

c) "Rooting in the sound" means to place ourselves in the sound, in the heart of the deity, where the moon disc is laid flat. As far as the Noble Tara is concerned, we visualize in the centre of the moon disc, the root-syllable TAM surrounded by the mantra letters OM TARE TOU TARE TOURE SOHA. The aim is to focus our attention on the mantra letters located in the heart of Tara on the moon disc. Now we are ready to recite the mantra.

4. Being-as-it-is of meditation

Being-as-it-is of meditation entails three aspects: being in the fire, being in the sound and conferring liberation through sound.

a) Being in the fire

In this special Tantra practice of the ritual action we generate ourselves as the deity. For example, if we choose Tara, in the middle of her breast, in her void body, we can see blazing flames and within the flames appear a moon disc flatly laid in the core of which we see the root-syllable TAM surrounded by OM TARE TOU TARE TOURE SOHA. It is called "being in the fire" or "abiding in flames". This visualization is an exert of mental clarity. Why do fire, flames, moon disc and mantra letters appear? They are symbolic representations, which enable us to realize the four activities of the Tantra practices:

a.1) Pacifying activity

The white light rays pacify, calm down and eliminate diseases, troubles and conflicts.

a.2) Increasing activity

The golden yellow light rays increase all positive and virtuous qualities and features.

a.3) Submitting and power activity.

The red light rays submit all kinds of entities, evil spirits and reluctant beings.

a.4) Destroying activity

The green light rays symbolize the destroying activity of the deity. The aim is to propel the consciousness of bad entities into a pure land, so that their capacity to impede is destroyed.

This fire visualization symbolizes the used means to achieve the four kinds of tantric activities.

b) Being in the sound

What does "being in the sound" mean? We have already begun to visualize the root-syllable TAM, then the mantra letters of the noble Tara. Now, we are pursuing the mantra recitation and our attention should focus on the produced sound. This method is a way to realize shine or calm abiding.

c) Conferring liberation through sound

Once the mantra recitation has begun and our attention is focusing on the sound, we can investigate about the nature of the sound. What is its nature? What is its essence? By progressively repeating the sound, we discover that the sound has an uncreated nature. We follow the sound up to the extreme and eventually, we discover that the sound is not self-existing. Sound is empty. This method enables us to realize vipasyana, (Tib. Lhaktong) or superior seeing.

5. Conduct (Tib. Chödpa)

The conduct implies here that practitioners carry out six activities in respect with:

a) Time

For example, there are special dates convenient for practicing, such as the eight or tenth of the Tibetan lunar month.

b) Food

It is recommended to take the three whites substances: butter, yoghurt and milk; the three sweet ones: honey, molasses and sugar; and to avoid meat, fish and onions.

c) Clothes

It is important to always wear impeccable, neat and simple

clothes. Do not wear second-hand, borrowed, torn out or dirty clothes.

d) Body and speech hygiene

Body and speech should be clean and neat. We should refrain from any offending words or insults.

e) Support

On the eighth of the Tibetan lunar month, we put a statue on our shrine, whatever material it is made of, bronze or stoneware, it does not matter. In front of the statue we dispatch the eight traditional offerings: twofold water, five offerings, (flowers, incense, light, fragrance, food) and sound offering through the shell. It is important to take care of the neatness of the shrine and the offerings.

f) Mantra repetition

The aim is to repeat the mantra in respect to the instructions given by the guru during the empowerment. The sound of the mantra should not be too loud, nor too low. It has to be audible for the practitioner, who is reciting it. Mantra recitation means "adoration" or "celebration" (Tib. Ngag pa). By intensively repeating the mantra during a retreat, we cultivate the sacred bond that has been set during the empowerment. It becomes deeper through practising.

A retreat can be conducted according to three references:

1. Duration or period of time

We can set a specific duration for our retreat, for example one week or ten days and we commit ourselves to stay in retreat for this given time. We do not leave before it is completed.

2. Amount of mantras to recite

We set the amount of mantra to recite and we stay in retreat as long as we have not attained this amount.

3. Signs of success

The time spent in retreat depends on signs and marks of success. Very often a retreat lasts six months. But after one month of sustained and intensive practice, if we have the vision of the practised deity, then we have completed our retreat.

6. Result. (Tib. Drebu)

The result is to obtain the state of the "three protectors of the three families", Chenrezig, Manjushree and Vajrapani, and more specifically to reach out this Enlightenment Land, which enables to achieve the vajra of these three protectors. Through Kriya Tantra, it is possible to realize ourselves in the deity dimension within one, three, seven lifetimes or at most within sixteen lifetimes.

Charya Tantra, the path of the behaviour

Presenting the nine progressive Yana in the perspective of the Nyingmapa tradition is not an easy task since they encompass all the Buddha's teachings classified in Sutras and Tantras. This is an immense topic. When the Baghavan passed away into Parinirvana, some of his brilliant and excellent disciples composed Shastras in such a great extent that His teaching was increased by many commentaries. The aim of this presentation is to give the quintessence of the Buddha's word as well as the major commentaries which have been written along the centuries in ancient India, then in Tibet and Nepal.

It is absolutely critical to have at least a good understanding of the three following fundamental points among the six linking points given for each vehicle, namely view, meditation and action. We should try to receive these teachings as if they were personal instructions conferred to us to enhance our own practice. We should strive to keep in mind the quintessence of view, meditation and action. If we project ourselves in the long term, not only in this present life, but rather thinking of our future lives, then we will be much more able to understand the deep meaning of this teaching. Hence it will enable us to defuse the karmic prints (Skt. Vasana, Tib. Bag-tchag), the finest veils which prevent the mind from recognizing its true nature, and are the main obstacles for beings living in confusion. This teaching, even if approached in a basic way, just for the enjoyment of discovering it, is already very much beneficial.

The specificity of Charya Tantra

View, conduct and fruition.

1. View is similar to the one of the Yoga Tantra presented hereafter.

2. Conduct is similar to the one of the previously presented Kriya Tantra.

3. Fruition: Practitioners of Charya Tantra aspire to realize ordinary and supreme siddhis.

The unique taste of Charya Tantra results from its special position half way between Kriya and Yoga Tantra.

Etymology

The groundwork of the Kriya Tantra practitioner is body activity including practices related to body and speech.

The groundwork of the Yoga Tantra practitioner is prajna yoga which is the main practice of the following Tantras. However it does not deal with prajna Rigpa, such as it is practised in Dzogchen. In prajna yoga, the issue of body hygiene is not of great importance.

The ground-work of the Charya Tantra practitioner takes place in an intermediate position. It conveys an adequate balance between the groundworks of the previous Tantras and the following Tantras. The behaviour (Skt. Charya) is moderate and balanced. Practices related to body and speech are as developed as those of prajna yoga. All practices are regarded on an equal level.

The six linking points

As far as Charya Tantra is concerned there are two changes in the traditional presentation of the six linking points. We will explain the view later on with the introduction of Yoga Tantra. Regarding conduct, it is similar to the one of Kriya Tantra and therefore we are not going to develop it here. So there are four linking points left that we are going to detail.

1. Entrance's door (Tib. Jugo)

The five prajna empowerments

a) Water empowerment
b) Silk cap empowerment
c) Vajra empowerment
d) Bell empowerment
e) Name empowerment

The first two ones, namely the water and silk cap empowerments are called "the true ones" since they are the foundations. The silk cap belongs to the eight silky ornaments worn by a Sambhogakaya. The vajra, bell and name empowerments are the three following ones. These five empowerments are the gateway which enables the practitioners to engage themselves on the Charya Tantra path.

a) Water empowerment

When the guru confers the water empowerment, he fertilizes the seeds which will enable the disciple to realize Dharmakaya. Thanks to this fertilizing, the seeds, which are already present in the disciple mind, will mature.

b) Silk cap empowerment

When the guru confers the silk cap empowerment, he fertilizes the seeds, which will enable the disciple to realize, in a more or less long term, the two forms of Rupakaya, the two formal bodies, namely the Sambhogakaya on a subtle level which deals with light body, and the Nirmanakaya, which deals with incarnation on a human level.

c) Vajra empowerment

When the guru confers the vajra empowerment, he fertilizes the seeds, which will enable the disciple to realize the two kinds of knowledge or prajna, which feature a fully awakened mind.

At first there is "the knowledge of what is, the way it is", namely the awareness of the absolute. Then, there is "the knowledge of everything that is appearing", this is the knowledge of the relative. These two knowledges arise simultaneously within an enlightened mind. There is no need to know first about the relative in order to shift to the absolute.

d) Bell empowerment

Vajrayana works with symbols to which the bell belongs. When the guru confers the bell empowerment, he fertilizes the seeds, which will enable the disciple to realize "the sixty qualities of the tuneful Brahma speech". It is about the immaculate speech of an enlightened being who will then in his turn awaken beings, since this speech is endowed with sixty qualities: it is powerful, smooth, tuneful and so forth...

e) Name empowerment

The aim of the name empowerment is to destroy any kind of karmic prints or traces, which grab us down into one birth or another into one of the three following realms: yearning or desire, with-form and without-form realms.

2. View (Tib. Tava)

We will detail the view in the Yoga Tantra later on.

3. Ethic (Tib.Tsültrim)

Ethic entails fourteen samayas to uphold. There are various degrees of graveness by not upholding these samayas. Different terms are used to graduate from the least to the gravest: "scratching", "damaging" and "sinking". There are some serious mistakes we should confess, since they can be the cause of sinking, which is very bad for the guru, the yidam and the practitioner.

a) The first ten samayas

The first ten samayas are the ten Pratimoksha vows, referring to the ten virtuous actions, such as the three positive actions of body, speech and mind. Usually it is expressed otherwise: « refraining from doing the three negative actions related to body, the four negative actions related to speech and the three negative actions related to mind, such as greed, nastiness and distorted or wrong views".

The teachings included in the three great progressive levels, which are Hinayana, Mahayana and Vajrayana have to be all integrated by practitioners. Scriptures say: «every single thing cultivated in the base moves then to the peak». We do not forget what has been the foundation before moving then to a higher level. Everything is kept; we are just adding on and adding on. The only change concerns the following designation: the Hinayana "vows" are then called "precepts" in Mahayana and "samayas" in Vajrayana.

We can already use the word «samaya» when we define the ethic in fourteen points of the Charya Tantra, since the practitioner has now entered into Vajrayana.

b) The four specific samayas

The eleventh samaya and first of the four specific samayas consists of not abandoning the excellent dharma.

The twelfth samaya and second of the four specific samayas consists of not abandoning the Bodhicitta, the Heart of Enlightenment.

The thirteenth samaya and third of the four specific samayas consists of not lacking generosity and offering dharma to beings.

The fourteenth samaya and last of the four specific samayas consists of not harming anyone.

All together they make fourteen sinking causes to avoid and they found the ethic of the Tantrika (Skt. Tantrika) of Charya Tantra.

4. Meditation. (Tib. Gompa)

Meditation practised in Charya Tantra is different from the one practised in Kriya Tantra.

In Kriya Tantra the relationship between yidam and practitioner looks like a king to his vassal or a master to his servant. It is not conceivable to be equally considered with the deity that is set on a pedestal. Through honouring the deity with various offerings, praises and above all showing our faith/trust and devotion we expect to receive accomplishments.

In Charya Tantra the yidam is perceived as a friend, an ally, a sister/brother, a relative or someone we are close to. By cultivating this kinship we can expect to realize siddhis. The relationship between the practised deity or wisdom being, (Skt. Jnanasattva, Tib. Yeshe Sempa) and the samaya being or promissing being (Skt. Samayasattva, Tib. Damtsig Sempa), namely the practitioner, is based on equality.

Meditation with and without sign

Two types of meditation are practised: with sign and without sign. The former one is called meditation of "entering into the location where the deity rises". This expression contains three notions: entering, location, and rise.

a) Meditation with sign

The aim is to generate the deity in front of us and then to visualize ourselves with the deity features. The deity visualization is a mental support. Meditation with sign also comprises the first letter and the second letter, the first base and the second base.

a.1) The first letter

We meditate ourselves as being emptiness, the absolute Bodhicitta. From that point arises the first letter which unfolds within spontaneity.

a.2) The second letter

The second letter conveys the relative Bodhicitta which appears as a flatly laid radiant white moon disc.

a.3) The first base

From this natural state of the relative Bodhicitta, which appears as a moon disc, we generate ourselves as a yidam.

a.3) The second base

From the first base, the deity in front of us appears like a reflection in a mirror: this is the second base. The point is not to do a drawing mental exercise, but simply to visualize the deity as being like a reflection in a mirror. From there we can start reciting the mantra with concentration, which means that we experience ourselves with the pure features of the deity, which is in front of us. The concentration associated with the mantra recitation will enable us to realize the siddhis related to the immaculate Body (Tib. Ku) of the deity, the siddhis related to the immaculate Speech (Tib. Sung) of the deity and the siddhis related to the Heart (Tib. Tuk), the awakened mind of the deity.

The two letters and the two bases are a meditation with signs or marks.

« Out of this letter, let's make another one! »

In a Tantra called "The perfect purification by Vairocana", we find the following expression: « Out of this letter, let's make another one! ». It is so codified that it is impossible to understand its meaning without the explanations of a guru. Actually, it means that from the first letter, namely emptiness, we should let the second letter arise, namely the relative. In respect to the first and second base it is said: « Out of this base, let's make another one! ». It means that from this first base, which consists of meditating ourselves as the yidam, we should let the second base appear, namely the meditated deity in front of us.

A fully justified "secret"

It is fully justified to talk about secret mantra as there is a real intention to keep secret all practices related to this path. In some extent, we have to deserve it. We have to be mature enough to be able to access to these three fundamental elements: empowerments that make us mature, teachings that liberate and transmissions (Tib. Lung) that make a support. It is a whole maturing process of the disciple who is empowered by the guru. During empowerment, there is a transfer: the blessings and grace of the master flow into the disciple. Some use the expression "power transmission". Through this transfer, the mind of the disciple ripens and rises from the ordinary usual level of the limited mental perceptions to another dimension, that of wisdom which is self-existing and self-radiating.

Among the three secret aspects, without going into details, we can mention for example the secret which forbids the conferring of deep instructions to those who are not ready to hear them and who might alter or distort them, and even get harmed.

What is the benefit, for example, to communicate, without any explanations, this teaching which is completely mysterious: « Out of this letter, let's make another one! »? The meaning of this sentence is totally unintelligible.

Only the master, while conferring the empowerment that ripens and the teaching that liberates, can communicate the meaning of the instructions he is giving to the disciple. Another example is this very sibylline phrase, which should not come to any ears and is a quotation of the Sutras, found in the Buddha's teachings: « Father and mother must be killed ». Here, the father refers to anger and mother to yearning. Expressed a little bit like a koan, the profound meaning of this phrase has to be explained by the master. Understanding mistakes may be very serious. By the same way, there is a whole set of codified messages, whose meaning can only be delivered by a guru. It can not be otherwise.

b) Meditation without sign

Meditation without sign refers to the meditation of "entering into the location where the deity rises".

This expression contains three: entering, staying in place, rising.

a) Entering

Entering means that the disciple understands that all living and manifested phenomena are not self-existing, are not independent entities. After a deep investigation, we do not find anything. This statement leads us to the essence of those phenomena, namely emptiness. Consequently, the disciple really understands that the whole reality, being alive or not, results from the great emptiness.

b) Staying in place

After investigation, the practitioner is getting familiar to the reality of emptiness. Then, he or she stays in the very heart of this realization, in a natural state and then rests there meditating.

c) Rising

"Rising" means here to "rise from a certain state". Once the practitioner has accessed to this understanding of the absolute and has remained stable within, then when he or she gets out of this natural state he or she will never sink again in an ordinary dualistic consciousness. Instead of that, the practitioner can better assess to which extent all beings wander in Samsara and enhance their confusion, since they can not realize emptiness. There is here a perfect link occuring between the knowledge of the absolute, namely the wisdom and this energy of love and compassion. As a matter of fact love and compassion result from realizing wisdom, from the statement that all beings are in confusion because they have not got a single clue about wisdom.

Therefore the purpose is to enter into this absolute dimension, to be at the heart of this understanding and to remain there. Then we can rise to the whole living world and look upon it with a fully compassionate look based on prajna and nurtured by wisdom and awareness. The function of this meditation with and without sign is to calm down all our thoughts, which are even at a subtle level still present in the first stage of the meditation with sign. This meditation is a skilful means to access to absolute Bodhicitta and remain there without any specific support. For this purpose, thoughts, even the subtlest ones, have to be absorbed.

5. Conduct (Tib. Tcheupa)

Conduct is similar to the one of a Kriya Tantra practitioner.

6. Result (Tib. Drebu) of the Charya Tantra is "the bhumi where the vajra of the four families can be held". It refers to the three families of Chenrezig, Manjushree and Vajrapani and the fourth family, namely the Jewel one (Skt. Ratna). It means that the Jewel family contains in essence the three families of the three protectors. This bhumi, even if it is not yet full Enlightenment, is already a kind of Enlightenment of the consciousness in this protecting dimension of the three existing realms: yearning or desire, form and without form.

At the crossroads: outer and inner yogas

Once we have reached out the Yoga Tantra, which is the last of the outer yogas, we have come to a crossroad. We can not say that the inner yoga of the three upper progressive vehicles (the three inner Tantras: Maha, Anu and Ati yoga) corresponds to the reality of Yoga Tantra but related to Kriya and Charya Tantra, it is a kind of inner yoga which starts to appear.

Towards the very deepest one

For most practitioners, the Buddha's teaching is introduced in progressive way, step by step, stages after stages. Considering the view according to these different stages starting at the first of the nine vehicles and ending up at the peak, namely Dzogchen, we are likely to say that we move along to the deepest stage.

For a practitioner of the first yana, the view is the realization of the non-self of persons. For a practitioner of the Maha yoga, the view goes far beyond the realization of the non-self of persons. The perception of the absolute is much deeper. By the same way, Dzogchen is the last of the nine yana and is the deepest one.

Nevertheless, for a given individual, what a so called inferior vehicle offers, may look deeper than what is offered by a so called superior vehicle.

Personal practice matters most

The nine yana offer a progression from the least deep to the deepest one. But in no case should we assert that this is fundamentally deeper, since what matters most is our personal practice, which makes all the difference.

If we consider the view according to the hearers and the view according to the Dzogchen practitioners, there is a huge gap between both of them. But for an individual, whose Buddha nature has been awakened to follow the hearer's path, the view of the non-self of persons is much deeper than the one proposed in Dzogchen.

What does deep mean?

Which instruction given to someone at a certain point on his or her path will be most beneficial, the deepest for him or her? Which one will give him or her key to open up? For a Shravaka, the view of the non-self of persons is much deeper than the view of the great uncreated space of Dzogchen. Thus, this practitioner feels really deeply concerned by the non-self of persons, and hence from that point he can open up.

What is deep for someone may not be deep for someone else

Within the absolute, the realization of the non-self of persons, the absence of a real "I" is deeper than the realization gained by refraining oneself from doing the ten negative actions. But for someone who is not engaged on a spiritual path, who has not even heard of the nine vehicles, instructions such as: not killing, not stealing and so forth will sound much deeper than the idea of a non-existing "I".

The depth must be considered from the absolute perspective as well as from the relative one. What is deep for someone is not deep for someone else.

An infinite number of paths for infinity of beings

The Buddha's teachings are of a great diversity. They are infinitely vast and complex. Why are they so complex? Two famous verses state: «As long as this great diversity of consciousness does not extinguish within Enlightenment, there will be as many spiritual paths offered as many sentient beings there are».

Buddha is fully awakened through the absolute reality. He accesses Unity. He takes into account the diversity of beings as far as their abilities, personality and karma are concerned. But there is also the strength of his past wishes, of his mind that has been lifetimes after lifetimes reincarnated as a Bodhisattva and has long cultivated the wish perfection: «May I continuously serve sentient beings in their multiple needs, under multiple aspects ».

Above all it is important to be clever, to discriminate what suits us from the basic presentation of the karma law, concentrated in the explanation of the ten virtuous deeds, up to the peak, namely Dzogchen. As we progress along the path, it is necessary to wonder what is essential for us to deepen among the three main principles of the practice: view, meditation or action.

Once we have experienced at least the non-self of persons, the next step arises quite naturally. The aim is not only to contemplate the absence of this illusory "I" but rather to discover what is hidden behind the representation of "I", and so forth. Our view is getting wider. Meditation consists of stabilizing ourselves within this view and our deeds will be the extension of it. We are asked to really deepen each step before switching to the next one, and so on, up to reach out Dzogchen. The Buddha's teachings are of an infinite number. There are many masters, many philosophical streams, and many different thinking schools. But if we continuously run from one to the other, though we will attend many teachings sessions, the result will be very limited on our own personal spiritual development, since we will not have been able to understand the innermost essence of the view, which is basically required in the practice and which is the foundation of our way of being in the world.

Like beggars collecting as much as possible

We will know about many things but ignore the most fundamental for our blossoming. We miss the essential by collecting teachings, empowerments and so on. Behind this outward show, we are like beggars.

Practitioners suffering from three kinds of loss

Expressed as a kind of joke, it is said that practitioners suffer from three kinds of loss:

1. Losing one's intelligence in scriptures

Too much memorizing too many scriptures makes our little intelligence disappear in studying.

2. Losing precepts through words we talk about the precepts instead of applying them. We are fine talkers. We get lost in triviality. We are supposed to put certain precepts into practice, and thus process to inner changes, but instead we sink into triviality.

3. Like molten metal...

The illustration of this truth is molten metal which falls down on the floor, still glowing, but after a while it becomes black iron. As practitioner we are supposed to start an inner process of transformation through applying precepts in our life, but because of laziness or intellectual argumentativeness, we fall to an ordinary level: what was glowing red becomes black and stiff.

In the training mind's precepts (Tib. Lo Djong), it is said: « What a fine figure they had when, fully satisfied, they were lying in the sun, but what a shabby figure they have when facing adversity! » We can see how we can amazingly be manifesting wisdom, like a great yogi, when we have a full stomach, but as soon as something turns wrong, we burst out of anger and we show another face!

Precepts of Kadampa masters

One precept of Kadampa masters state: «Meditating patience does not mean disappearing far away in the forest, whereby there is none, with whom we may have a conflictual relationship, but instead it involves facing the conflictual beings we may encounter ». Practising calm abiding in a remote place, in the mountain or in the very core of the forest and gaining there a certain mental peace, but then being back in town with an agitated mind is the sign that we have not reached any stable state. We have not realized neither shine nor lhaktong. We can also quote another Kadampa precept: «Whatever we do in this lifetime, in any of the four situations, by walking, sitting, standing or lying, everything must be meant to become a cause of Enlightenment».

Everything must be used as a means to Enlightenment. If there is on one hand the practice we are doing with attention and regularity in a remote place, and on the other hand other activities, which seem to us less interesting, then we are mistaken. There must always be union of meditation and action.

The eighty prayers forms of a Bodhisattva

In the eighty prayers forms a Bodhisattva learn in the seventh prayer Paramita (Tib. Mönlam), we can find several interesting examples, even if a little trivial, but we should consider them in their context. When a Bodhisattva urinates, he thinks that he is offering his urine to the greedy ghosts (Skt. Preta, Tib. Yi-dag), invisible beings who are in a mental body and steadily experience the suffering of thirst. May this urine be used to quench their thirst! Urinating becomes an offering. When a Bodhisattva goes to the toilets to defecate, he thinks that he offers his faeces to the white worms. This shows that even the most trivial daily deeds can be part of a continuous and spontaneous offering practice.

The way we go to bed

In all circumstances, there is a way to live while being fully connected to the Whole. It is very important to pay attention to the way we go to bed. If, for instance, at this moment we give free rein to desire and attachment or to anger, our whole sleep will be contaminated by these energies. As opposed to this, if we say a simple prayer as will do a Bodhisattva, totally impregnated of this loving-kindness energy, wishing that all beings get freed of suffering and that they awaken to their true nature, our sleep will benefit from this Bodhicitta energy. Our sleep will produce positive energy at a subtle level. Therefore the way we go sleeping is critical.

The tenth Yana, the Yana of great spontaneity!

This is a humoristic point! If these teachings belong to the great set of the nine gradual vehicles, what has just been said is actually the tenth gradual vehicle of great spontaneity: the personal Yana of Khenpo Chimed Rinpoche!

Yoga Tantra, the union path

A quotation by Tsongkhapa

While entering the path of the hearer, it is very important to be in the right state of mind and to generate the right motivation. It is useful to quote these words by Tsongkhapa, who was one of the three great emanations of Manjushree in Tibet: «At the very beginning, if there is a noble and generous thought, in this lifetime and in the future ones it can only produce excellent things».

Reflecting about it in a spiritual perspective, it can only lead us to the excellence of the three learning paths (preparation, application and vision) then to the double path of meditation, where we can then move along the ten bodhisattva bhumis.

Such a seed-like motivation can only give birth to an immense tree bearing excellent fruits. Similarly, this noble and generous thought can only produce the excellence of the five paths and ten bhumis, in this lifetime as well as in the future ones.

If, at a spiritual level, such an excellence arises, favourable conditions for practicing naturally appear and are of great help on the paths without any necessary striving to get them. However, a bad fundamentally self-oriented thought, or a conflictual or despising thought towards other people can only generate bad results in this lifetime or in the future ones, for ourselves as well as for other people. At first, this negative thought seems to be meaningless, but as time goes by, it will keep on growing and eventually will bring us much suffering while sinking.

On the spiritual path, it is necessary to care in all circumstances, either in the first stage, called practice of attention and listening, as well as in the second one, the practice of reflection, or the third essential one called the meditation to keep this purity of thought and above all loving kindness and noble heart alive and present. This practice is experienced within by a feeling of great spontaneous generosity. It is individually carried out, but it encompasses all beings. If we are able to awaken ourselves, we will be able to bring something really positive to others.

The early morning positive thought

When getting up in the morning, it is important to be in an excellent state of mind, in a deep-hearted state of generosity. Generating generous thought has nothing to do with being male or female, wealthy and powerful or poor and little fortunate. Whatever our mind is like, the strength of our thought enables us, even if we are of the lowest condition of life, to be generous and lavish in our wish for happiness for all beings. This noble thought is like the foundations of a house. Whatever the house looks like, whether it be a one or two-storey house or at street level, the foundations are crucial. Similarly, on the spiritual path, whatever yana we have been engaged into, whether we have reached Vajrayana or whether we find ourselves at a standstill on the path, what makes the construction stable is a result of our generous mind and thoughts. This nobleness must be there from the very beginning. If it is lacking, it is very difficult to be considered a spiritual being. Certainly, we can practice meditation and may have reached a certain level of concentration, but without deep-hearted generosity, it is not possible to be a genuine spiritual practitioner.

There must be this loving generosity, even if attaining Full Enlightenment seems to be beyond our capacities. This deep-hearted generosity is fundamental because it is creating inner well-being and peace. This very single reason is sufficient in itself. It is easy to understand this by looking at examples around us and experiencing it ourselves. If we care being in this natural generosity and not in a superficial way, it brings relaxation, peace and happiness. It is positive for ourselves. If we are in this generous state of mind, other people will be sensible to this kindness; they will appreciate it, smile back to us and be more positive towards us. When someone has a heart of stone or is heartless, not caring to cultivate this generosity of mind because of their being too ensnared by selfishness, then that individual can only think and care about himself or is always trying to take advantage of others. However hard this person tries to utter friendly words, they will remain without effect, since from the deepest part of his heart, there is no genuine joy of living nor life's power, nor true generosity and kindness. Hence his words will remain meaningless.

For everyone except my neighbour

We may be proud of repeatedly uttering words like wishing to attain Full Enlightenment for the sake of "all sentient beings", but sometimes we actually innerly mean "all beings except" my neighbour. In this case, it is better to start here and now with the people close to us, and then to widen it out to others.

The difference between a holy person and an ordinary one

What makes the difference between a holy person and an ordinary one? The difference does not come from flesh, nor from the skin nor from the bones. It does not result from any title, from a nice face or a whiter or darker skin. Not at all! What makes the difference is spontaneous heart kindness. We can paraphrase the prayers words (Tib. Mönlam) that the dakini, Yeshe Tsogyal, uttered to the great master

Padmasambhava. At one time, she asserted that with this heart nobleness, which is the expression of bodhicitta, it is possible to subjugate beings. Subjugation! Not in a worldly meaning, but rather in a spiritual meaning. It means guiding people to get out of their bad tendencies to open them up to their positive abilities. Beings can be inwardly converted, in the noble meaning of the word, not through aggressive means, but rather through the power of love. Then, the dakini Yeshe Tsogyal said that thanks to the jewel of natural wisdom we can open up the door to the heart. And in the following verses she continued: «Through this jewel of natural wisdom, which dwells within ourselves, it is possible to benefit beings and to bring them welfare and happiness». Therefore, we can notice that the gateway or entrance door opens up our heart, which leads us to active wisdom, and so gives us the capacity to act for the sake of beings.

Inner conversion

Converting people in the noble sense of the word means that beings, who may have been considered as enemies or opposed to a spiritual path or to a master, can be inwardly converted through the power of a master's love. A conversion is happening and it is irreversible. When a being is inwardly converted through the power of love of a great enlightened master, this conversion is absolutely irreversible. People's tendencies come and go, but eventually we have to contemplate the transient aspect of everything that was born and appears. Someone, who was the closest person to us at a given time can become an enemy, and someone, with whom we may have today a conflicting relationship may become later very close to us. People who were at a given time close can move totally apart at some other time. But when the power of love is really efficient, feelings can be deeply changed from within. This is an irreversible process.

The three levels of the nine progressive yana

Reducing these nine progressive yana to three great yana is a way of taking into account three levels of spiritual maturity among beings. Are defined as "superior" beings, those who are very advanced, then in second position come those beings, who are in an intermediate stage on their spiritual path, and finally there are beginners.

The first three yana are contained in the first great vehicle that is called the "rising vehicle through emanations".

The following three yana are contained in the "knowledge vehicle through asceticism".

Within each of these three great yana, there are also three different levels: a lower, a medium and a higher level.

For example, as far as the "knowledge vehicle through asceticism" is concerned, there are three outer Tantras, each of which is meant for practitioners at different levels: Tantras of ritual action are given to practitioners of lower-medium level, Tantras of behaviour are given to practitioners of intermediate-medium level and Tantras of Maha yoga are meant for practitioners of higher-medium level.

We will now deal with the final stage of the second great vehicle, that is to say, Yoga Tantra, intended for practitioners of higher-medium level. What is Yoga Tantra about? Through the grace of the wisdom that comes from realizing the absolute, one also realizes that each and every living creatures, whether they be tangible or not, is totally deprived of self-existence and the whole relative dimension is perceived as the deity.

Being in the excellence of thought

This operating wisdom leads yogis or yoginis to consider that every single thing within the relative world is unfolding as the deity. This is the innermost essence of Yoga Tantra.

This state is called "realizing the fruit" or otherwise known as being in the state of "excellence of thought". Not realizing this state means being in "bad thoughts". These words of "bad" or "excellent thoughts" should not be understood here in their usual meaning, but rather as a kind of magical understanding of what "experiencing" or "not experiencing" Enlightenment means. These are "higher" words. For a yogi, "being in good thoughts" means experiencing this realization; whereas "not being in good thoughts" means not experiencing this realization. When being not in the core of this wisdom, the yogi has no chance of realizing Enlightenment.

Etymology

Why do we talk about Yoga Tantra? What does this word "yoga" refer to? If we compare this third class of Tantras with the two previous ones, where we were mostly insisting on body and speech, above all the yogi is here concerned with the "insight view", namely the pure view of wisdom.

The six linking points

1. Entrance's door (Tib. Jugo)

The entrance's door is similar to the one of Charya Tantras, based on five knowledge empowerments, except that within Yoga Tantra, there is a sixth empowerment called "empowerment by the vajra master".

These five empowerments of knowledge are really the entrance door into Vajrayana. They are as essential in the three more recent schools, that is in the Kagyüpa, Sakyapa and Gelugpa schools, as they are in the ancient Nyingmapa school. Within these five major schools of tantric Buddhism we find the five empowerments of prajna, which are displayed in exactly the same way.

Five empowerments of the disciple

Generally, speaking about these five empowerments of

knowledge refers to the empowerments of the disciple. Their aim is to purify the three doors of the disciple -body, speech and mind-, and to have them ripen.

Why is it necessary to purify the doors of the disciple and to have them mature? Since we are ordinary beings, our karma is impure. All these accumulated karmas are impure because they have originally been distorted by the illusory notion of "I". If, at an early stage, the master does not, symbolically and on a subtle level take care to purify the three doors of the disciple and have them mature, there will be no possible way for the disciple to get into the mandala, there will be no possible view, through the eye of wisdom, upon the mandala of the palace, and even less chance to be able to consider the deities as pure unfolding of wisdom.

Entering into the mandala

There are four steps to go through in order to get into the mandala, even before we receive the water empowerment.

1. Step one

First, we enter into the vajra space of the mandala. Perceptions here are obviously not ordinary and are unusual.

2. Step two

We commit ourselves to uphold vows and samayas.

3. Step three: the coming down of wisdom beings.

Our master prompts us to visualise ourselves as the deity. He explains how to sit properly in order to make the winds circulate easily and how to leave our breathing in its natural state, how to rest our consciousness like a slack sea, which the moon and the stars can perfectly reflect in. From that point, the true deity and its surroundings can fall down into us, like wisdom rain, and melt into us like snow flakes would fall down into a lake.

4. Step four

Before receiving this water that will bind us to the deity, we are given a real or symbolic flower. We hold it with our fingertip and then we let it drop onto the mandala that is presented to us on a tray. The place, where the flower falls, indicates to us which mandala family we belong to, whether it is Vairocana, Akshobya, Ratnasambhava, Amitabha, or Amoghasiddhi. By then, we are given the water contained in the second vase, the vase of the assembly of deities, in which all deities are present in a luminous and radiating manifestation. As we are now connected to our Buddha family, while we are receiving this water, our ordinary perception of ourselves is totally vanishing and we become like water poured into water. We become one with the immaculate body, speech and enlightened mind of the main deity and of the assembly of deities.

Five empowerments of knowledge

1. Water empowerment
2. Silk cap empowerment
3. Bell empowerment
4. Vajra empowerment
5. Name empowerment

1. Water empowerment or vase empowerment

Why do we talk about water empowerment or sometimes also called "vase empowerment"? Thanks to the master's power of concentration the empowerment vase, (Tib. Bumpa) which is used as a symbolic support, is perceived as being the mandala of the deities' palace. Thus, the water that is going to be given to the disciples to purify them, symbolizes the inhabitants of this palace, namely the whole gathering of deities. The master's power of concentration turns this water into the wisdom energy of the deities and the water turns into crystal clear water, which can purify us.

At the beginning, when the first Tibetan masters conferred empowerments in the Western countries, and especially when they did this vase empowerment, they used to put the vase on the disciples' head, then they poured some water into the palm of their hands, but then people stared at this water, wondering what to do with it. Sometimes there were some quite funny episodes.

The proper way to receive this water is to present our left hand, which is the hand of wisdom, then receive the water and to drink half of it. While drinking it, we think that it symbolizes the very essence of the mandala's deities, whose empowerment is being conferred. Then, while swallowing the water, we think that it really possesses the power to purify and mature our body, our speech and our mind. At that very moment, and this is the critical point, whereby the true power of the empowerment really operates: we in fact become indivisible and inseparable from these deities, and at a subtler level we come into contact again with our true primordial nature, which is of the same nature as these deities.

Saying good bye to Samsara

Then, we throw the other remaining half of the water over our back, which means that we are leaving behind the three realms of Samsara. As we have now established this connection with the deities, how could we keep on living in the Samsara any longer? While throwing the second part of the remaining water behind us, we think that we are saying good bye to Samsara. The master, who is conferring the empowerment, uses two vases: the activity vase containing the crystal clear purifying water and the assembly vase, which is experienced by the master as really being the palace of the deity, containing the assembly of deities. When we are offered the water from the second vase, we must think that our three doors are ripening and becoming inseparable from the immaculate body, speech and awakened mind of all Buddhas and of our master.

2. Silk cap empowerment

The silk cap empowerment entails five empowerments,

namely the cap empowerment of the five dhyani Buddhas: Vairocana, Akshobya, Ratnasambhava, Amitabha and Amoghasiddhi.

3. Bell empowerment

While receiving the bell empowerment, we are receiving the empowerment of the bell that the main deity holds in its left hand or in one of its left hands. Thus, we are directly introduced on a subtle level to the living speech of the deity, which is a wisdom speech, even if it can not be heard.

4. Vajra empowerment

While receiving the vajra empowerment, we are receiving the empowerment of the vajra that is held by the main deity who may become the yidam of the practitioner. Receiving this empowerment means innerly receiving, within this primordially pure dimension, the grace and blessing of what is, such as it is, namely the grace of the "absolute", and the grace of every single phenomenom, that is the unfolding of the relative world. This empowerment enables us to open up to the absolute reality, which is the main deity.

5. Name empowerment

While throwing the flower into the symbolic mandala we are presented to, we are receiving a name, which is associated to one of the five Buddha families, namely Vairocana or the family with the eightfold rayed-wheel, Akshobya or the vajra family, Ratnasambhava or the jewel family, Amitabha or the lotus family, and Amoghasiddhi or the karma family also defined as the double vajra family.

These five empowerments of knowledge, also called "empowerments of the disciple" are presented here in a very simplified way. Their main function is to help the disciple mature. Among the recent schools (Kagyüpa, Sakyapa and Gelugpa) as well as in the ancient Nyingmapa school, there is no difference in the way these empowerments are conferred by the corresponding masters. The way to proceed is exactly the same. This empowerment is the basis, the necessary condition to go through to gain access to the empowerments that will follow later, whether it be an empowerment related to Kriya, Charya, Maha yoga, or to others. This name empowerment is essential since, if the master does not prepare the disciple, nor purify him, the disciple will not be able to receive the main empowerment.

Empowerment by the vajra master

The empowerment conferred by the vajra master makes the Yoga Tantra superior to the two other outer Tantra classes. This empowerment conveys the highest level in the Yoga Tantra.

The empowerment by the vajra master contains six empowerments:

a) No-return empowerment
b) Secret empowerment
c) Permission empowerment
d) Prophecy empowerment
e) Liberation empowerment
f) Exhortation empowerment

We will only explain the no-return and secret empowements.

a) No-return empowerment

The no-return empowerment commits ourselves to uphold the samayas, which are going to link us to the immaculate bodies of the master and yidam, to the immaculate speech of the master and yidam, as well as to the immaculate and awakened mind of the master and yidam. This samaya commits ourselves to always keeping the pure vision towards these three principles.

b) Secret empowerment

The secret empowerment refers to the precious empowerment of speech. At a given point, we are outside the mandala, usually at the East gate of the mandala, and the vajra master is going to enable us to get into the mandala.

Thus, we secretly enter the mandala. This so-called secret empowerment refers to the way we are entering into the mandala.

How is the secret entrance into the mandala occuring?

First of all, we prostrate ourselves, then we recite the sevenfold-branch prayer, namely:

1. prostrations

2. offering all our possessions and goods

3. confession

4. rejoicing

5. request to the masters to turn the Dharma wheel

6. request to the masters to remain in Samsara to help people

7. final dedication of all merits.

Then, we have a kind of vision of the deities' palace. What is called mandala, encompasses the deities' palace itself, as well as the assembly of the deities, who are part of it. Once they have been honored by offerings and prostrations, they appear to us through a wisdom unfolding. From that point on, we go backwards along the same path: from the wisdom unfolding we trace the way back to the very essence of the absolute, which is the source of these unfolding deities.

This empowerment is secret because it is far beyond any ordinary thought and thinking. It is ineffable. During this empowerment, we may be able to perceive the colourful and majestic unfolding of all deities, which is the innermost essence of the absolute.

Altogether, we have eleven empowerments composed of five empowerments of knowledge and six empowerments of the vajra master: they are the entrance doors to Yoga Tantra.

2. View (Tib. Tava)

The very essence of the non ordinary view in Yoga tantra is to experience, from the ground of the wisdom that realizes the absolute, all the relative world as a deity unfolding. The non ordinary view is also characterized by a lack of marks and signs. For the yogi, it means that the whole unfolded reality is experienced as being part of the space of the absolute reality, namely the vajra space.

Once we have been introduced to the vajra space, the ordinary perceptions we have had about a tangible, inanimate world, made out of four elements and of living creatures that result from contaminated karmas, are completely eliminated. What now determines perceptions is wisdom. The impure world could only exist because there had been an impure view on top of it. Once we have been introduced to this wisdom dimension, no longer can we have an impure view upon it. The view is transmuted. The world of elements dissolves to become a space of light and sentient beings are perceived as deities unfoldings. This is how the energy of the view is characterized in Yoga Tantra.

Ethic deals with upholding samayas. Within Vajrayana we do not talk about vows, nor precepts, but about samaya. There are two sorts of samayas: the "general" and the "specific"ones.

The four general samayas are:

1. Generating Bodhicitta
2. Upholding the special learning process of ethic
3. Upholding the special learning process of concentration
4. Upholding the special learning process of wisdom

Ethic leads to concentration which leads to wisdom.

The four specific samayas shared out among the five Buddha families.

The three samayas related to Vairocana, in the Centre, are:

1. Generating Bodhicitta
2. Upholding the ethic
3. Taking refuge

The four samayas related to Akshobya, in the East, are:

1. Never being separated from the vajra or from one picture of it

2. Never being separated from the bell or from one picture of it

3. Relying upon the practice of the yidam

4. Relying upon the lama

The four samayas related to Ratnasambhava, in the South, are:

1. Materiel offering

2. Dharma offering

3. Protection offering, helping others to be fearless

4. Love offering, a mother-like love to her child, loving-kindness offering.

The only samaya related to Amitabha, in the West, is:

1. Being involved in every vehicle without letting one aside, pretending it would be of lower level.

The two samayas related to Amoghasiddhi, in the North, are:

1. Honouring the Three Jewels with offerings

2. Practising carefully at any time and whatever circumstances occur.

Concerning the upholding of the ethic, there is no distinction between the three recent schools (Kagyüpa, Sakyapa and Gelugpa) and the ancient school (Nyingmapa). Whatever school we belong to or are connected to, it is important to know about these samayas, so as to be able to uphold them.

Within the very heart of Vajrayana take place the victorious of the five families, the five dhyani Buddhas. These are general yidams common to all schools of tantric Buddhism. Each school has got specific deities such as Vajrakilaya, Hayagriva or Hevajra, for example, but the five dhyani Buddhas always remain in the very heart of all schools. From these five dhyani Buddhas arise all the other deities.

At the heart essence of the Vajrayana practice, we must cultivate the deep link to the five dhyani Buddhas. For example, Vajrapani, who is one of the three protectors of the three realms, actually is Vajrasattva, also called Akshobya. For example, Dordje Chönu, the young vajra, also named Vajrakilaya (Tib. Dordje Purba) is the wrathful aspect of Vajrasattva, who is a peaceful deity. In essence, Manjushree is Ratnasambhava. Amitabha, the Buddha of infinite beauty and radiance, as dhyani Buddha of the lotus family, which is the family of the immaculate speech, appears with the features of the horse-headed Hayagriva, when he is wrathful. We could mention other deities associated to Vairocana, Ratnasambhava or Amoghasiddhi. The five dhyani Buddhas represent the field of manifestation, whereby all the peaceful or wrathful deities may appear.

4. Meditation (Tib. Gompa)

Within Yoga Tantra meditation is practised with signs or without signs.

Meditation with signs

Meditation with signs comprises five generating aspects to purification called "five awakenings for a total purification of prints". Through this purification, each and every print and trace is being cleansed away. The Kyerim practice, which is the generation stage of the deity, consists of purifying the four ways of birth: through a womb, from an egg, in dampness/warmth or mould, and at last instantaneous birth or "miraculous birth".

Within Yoga Tantras, Kyerim enables us to experience ourselves as the deity, however the level is not subtle enough to delete all imprints that have led us to be reborn through one of these four ways and so kept us going round and round the wheel within the different samsaric worlds.

Five generating aspects to purification

1. Awakening from the base that is emptiness

2. Awakening from the lotus seat
3. Awakening from the root-letter
4. Awakening from the ritual objects held by the deity
5. Awakening from the whole immaculate body of the deity

To help you understand how to practise these meditations within the Yoga Tantras, I am going to explain each aspect of Kyerim through the example of Tara, as Yidam.

1. Awakening from the base that is emptiness

When we practise the Venerable Tara, we firstly take refuge in her and then we generate Bodhicitta. Then, we develop this kind of mental clarity that enables us to become aware that all phenomena are part of the great emptiness and, thus to find ourselves in this natural state of emptiness. Through practising such a meditation, not a fabricated but a really experienced one, these prints (Skt. Vasana, Tib. Bag-tchag), as well as every kind of clinging that makes us believe in any kind of existence, in dualism and in the eternity of phenomena, are being purified. This first stage of the meditation enables us to purify all imprints that are related to eternalism, that is to say the belief that all phenomena would have an intrinsic and eternal existence. The four following practices aim at purifying the opposite extreme belief, namely all imprints related to nihilism.

2. Awakening from the lotus seat

During meditation, from this natural state of emptiness that is the base, spontaneously arises an eightfold petal lotus, whose clarity is cultivated. This meditation becomes the cause for the realization of pure bhumis and pure lands. The mere clear representation of the eightfold petal lotus will once, when it ripens, turn into a real pure land. Contemplating the lotus is the cause that will make a pure land appear which is a perfect location to be in. This location is not only meant for ourselves. This pure land is meant to welcome all beings, all kind of living creatures. The eightfold petal lotus is the cause for a luminous and radiant place to welcome all beings that long to awaken themselves. Therefore, we use the expression "Awakening from the lotus seat", on which the deity is sitting, but this is the second step in the meditation process.

3. Awakening from the root-letter

The root-letter is in essence the immaculate speech of the deity.

In the core of the lotus, on the stamen, there is the green root-letter TAM of the Venerable Tara. Having this clear vision of the root-letter means to "awaken from the root-letter that is the immaculate speech". Focusing by this way on the root-letter of the deity creates the cause that will enable us in the future to turn the dharma wheel for the sake of all beings.

4. Awakening from the ritual objects held by the deity

For example, awakening thanks to the vajra or the bell, or other ritual objects according to the practised deity. These ritual objects symbolize the awakened mind of the deity. With Tara, there is no real ritual object. Tara holds the stem of a blue lotus flower called Upala in her left hand. The green root-letter TAM, that stands in the heart of the eightfold petal lotus, is transformed into a blue lotus flower Upala. This clear vision of the blue lotus flower creates the cause that will make the dharma wheel continuously turn within an eternal stream-like period of time. It is not about an eternal period of time without any changes, but literally speaking, it deals with "this eternal ever changing time that will last up to the end of Samsara".

5. Awakening from the whole immaculate body of the deity

The TAM is transformed into a blue lotus and the blue lotus is then turned into the whole immaculate body of the Venerable Tara. This pure and luminous vision of the Venerable Tara enables to create the cause of the realization of the perfection of the master and of his surroundings.

These five generating phases are applied for every practice deity, may it be Manjushree, Chenrezig or Hayagriva, etc. The root-letter and the ritual object vary according to the deity, but the principle remains alike. Each time we have to go through five stages.

These five steps within meditation, where we clearly visualise ourselves as the deity are sealed with the four seals.

The four seals

1. The seal of the immaculate body of the deity

2. The seal of the immaculate speech of the deity

3. The seal of the samayas related to the awakened mind of the deity

4. The seal of the activity through giving out and reabsorbing luminous rays.

For example the luminous rays radiate from Tara's breast to honour all Buddhas with offerings, to purify all beings and to save them. Then, these luminous rays come back, filled with the Buddha's grace and blessings and merge into Tara's heart.

The very essence of the meditation of a Yoga Tantra consists of, on the base of these five sorts of awakening, of having the experience that we are the deity (the first seal), reciting the mantra (the second seal), upholding the samayas of the awakened mind of the deity (the third seal) and of the emission and re-absorption of luminous rays filled with grace and blessings (the fourth seal).

By this way, our meditation is sealed with the four seals.

Meditation without signs

Meditation without signs consists of meditating the great emptiness.

5. Conduct (Tib. Chödpa)

Conduct consists of paying attention to body hygiene,

cleanness, diet, merely considering them as allies, without any tensed grasping on these issues.

6. Result (Tib. Drebu)

The result of a practitioner of the two previous Tantras consists of realizing the land of the three protectors of the three realms within Kriya Tantra, the land enabling to possess the vajra of the four Buddhas' families within Charya Tantra. The result of a Yoga Tantra practitioner consists of holding the vajra of the five, and not the four Buddhas' families, namely adding the karma family related to Amoghasiddhi.

Holding the vajra of the five families

A Yoga Tantra practitioner, who has come to the end of the path, has reached out "the land that is holding the vajra of the five families". Within the previous tantras, the Charya tantras, the aim is to reach out "the land that is holding the vajra of the four families".

If we realize the vajra family, will it mean that we might realize at the same time the other families? Yes, indeed! Because this land, that we have attained once we have completed the whole Yoga Tantra, actually comprises the five families.

Maha yoga, the path of the great union

Listening to Dharma teachings requires necessarily to be in the right state of mind and to generate the right motivation. It means to look upon all beings with love and compassion and to take into account their continuous sufferings. The more compassion we can feel towards beings, the more our motivation and determination to awaken ourselves grows and ripens. We long to attain Enlightenment to be able to set beings in the profound nature of Samantabhadra, the primordial Buddha, the state of Full Enlightenment. It is important to develop a double motivation: the motivation of the Mahayana basic principle, namely Bodhicitta, which is ocean-like vaste and profound, intended to pour love to the infinite multitude of beings, and secondly the Vajrayana specific motivation, which aims at developing a vision of infinite purity thanks to the great diversity of skilful means available within that particular vehicle. We must be moved by this infinite love towards beings and put a pure and immaculate look upon all living creatures and beings. Led by this compassionate and open mind we have become a proper receptacle for the teachings. Moved by this kind of motivation, we can really be attentive to what is following.

We have already come through the first six yana, gathered into two vehicles, "the rising vehicle through emanations" and "the knowledge vehicle through asceticism". We are now going to deal with the first among the three vehicles of the inner Tantras called "the transcending vehicle through skilful means" included in the secret circle (cf. page 11).

The three inner Tantras

The first inner Tantra or Maha yoga is intended for individuals endowed with lower faculties, the second inner Tantra for individuals with medium faculties and the third inner Tantra for individuals with upper faculties, namely people who can easily get the dimension that is far beyond any kind of mental understanding.

Upper faculties should not be understood as special qualities gained by a long scholarship, a deep practice of attention, awareness or reflection, nor as very sharp intellectual capacities, nor as any ability to fastly grasp a reality that can not be seized by ordinary mental perceptions. This notion of "upper faculties" can be explained by four aspects. The first one refers to "trust/faith", the second one to "admiration", which is a genuine capacity to appreciate what is particularly high. The third aspect deals with upholding samayas. The practitioner cares about to properly uphold the samayas that are always linked to a higher empowerment. The fourth aspect is concerning "pure vision".

Attending teachings on inner Tantras is allowed provided that one has received a Tantra empowerment. Once we are engaged into this approach, it is absolutely necessary to be moved by trust/faith, to remain open-minded so as to be able to receive the teachings with our heart and not with our intellect that is likely to judge. We must have pure vision.

Trust and faith, admiration and pure vision ought to be applied towards the Three Jewels, as well as the practised deity, the assembly of yidams, the dakinis, the dharmapalas, namely the dharma protectors, and obviously towards our root master(s) and the gurus of the lineage.

The sound of the drilling machine

The specific feature of Vajrayana is to plunge ourselves into a reality that is far away from the ordinary reality shaped by our ordinary mental. Staying in the spirit of the samayas means "practising the three applications". Once we are in the post-meditation stage, the first application consists of linking all experienced visual perceptions to the body of the deity, to the body of the masters, to the body of the dakinis, and so forth. The second application consists of linking all audible sounds to a variation in the mantra of the practised deity. Even if this sound, for example, sounds like the drilling machine we are now hearing... The third application refers to the thoughts that may arise in our mind, and that are not perceived in an ordinary way, but are linked to the awakened mind of the master and of the deity. We experience the thoughts as being a distraction or an entertainment of the awakened mind of the deity, namely of the Dharmakaya. By this way, we can cultivate the pure vision and we can nurture our trust and faith that is far beyond the ordinary perceptions.

Vajra brothers and sisters

We ought never to give up the trust/faith/devotion towards the guru, who introduces the disciples to the path of secret mantras. One should never abandon the trust in the dharma, this corpus of instructions for the practice of Vajrayana or secret mantras. Nor never giving up trust in the ones who are our vajra brothers and sisters, that is to say the people, with whom we have been together conferred important empowerments by the same master. Disciples, who have together received within the same mandala the same empowerments become vajra brothers and sisters. This instruction can be very easily forgotten and the trend to judge and condemn others may soon occur, if we are not careful. We must strive to cultivate this pure vision, not only towards the master, but also towards our vajra brothers and sisters, who are moving along the same path.

Giving up pride

Moreover, it is necessary to give up any kind of pride.

If pride is already deeply rooted, it may be too late, since it is commonly said that a proud person will always be the last one to recognize his or her own pride. One should never devote to pride or to any form of arrogance concerning, for example, our capacity to listen to teachings or to put them into practice. If there is not a minimum of quality, there is no point being arrogant about anything. But, particularly from that minimum of quality we have been able to develop through erudition, or even more insidiously, through a certain experience, the true poison appears when, starting to think we are superior to others, we become really arrogant. Bumptiousness is going to spoil everything. We should not give free rein to it. As soon as arrogance begins to appear, we should be careful enough not to give rise to it. When pride starts to have a certain power, the practitioner can not develop any admiration towards the master, nor towards the vajra brothers and sisters, nor even towards that excellent Dharma.

Sitting straightforward on the floor

In the Eastern culture, people care to sit as close to the floor as possible, or even to sit on the floor, and they do not seek to have a throne. Innerly, qualities such as humbleness and modesty are cultivated. Even if we have received many instructions, some of which may be very secret and restricted to few disciples, even if we have gained a certain quality of practice and level of experience, the best and easiest thing to do to avoid being affected by pride, which is like the shadow of ego, is to remain rooted in our determination to attain Enlightenment. As long as Enlightenment has not manifested yet, there is no use lingering over these little qualities that might have been developed along the path. As long as the five poisons such as desire and attachment, pride, jealousy, hatred and ignorance are not totally eliminated, we should not satisfy ourselves with few scattered qualities. If we are in such a state of mind, it will be impossible to become a victim of pride.

However, when pride is present, receiving, generating or maintaining pure vision is unconceivable towards the master, as well as to the vajra brothers and sisters. In that case we are likely to think that our realization is higher. In this Tibetan Buddhist tradition, we insist a lot on that point: pride is our worst enemy. A Tibetan saying tells that a peaceful, smooth and kind mind is the sign of a relatively advanced practise of attention and mindfulness. At the beginning, the mind looks rather like a devil, a wild animal, then it is submitted. The well-known conflicting emotions that are desire, rejection and ignorance gradually decrease, a little bit like someone, who would slowly lose weight.

Like a wolf in a sheepfold...

Do not imagine that pride could bring with it obstacles for memorising scriptures or entering into high studies, not at all! The problem is that pride rather looks like a wolf in a sheepfold. The sheep are the qualities and pride is the wolf. Have you got it? However, it does not mean that we are here only a bunch of proud people and that we would deserve to make some more prostrations... no, no, do not worry! There is nothing special neither implied...nor suggested.

Vajra pride

Ordinary pride should not be mistaken with "adamantine pride" also called "vajra pride". This kind of pride represents the trust we feel of being the deity.

Conflicting emotions related to the four lineages

Within the Nyingmapa tradition, the devotion towards Guru Rinpoche and the emanations of Guru Rinpoche, such as Dudjom Rinpoche, Dielgo Khyentse Rinpoche, is immense. They were great beings, who had a mystic consort.

Some other Nyingmapas eventually have wondered why they could not have one too. They think: "why not me?"

On one hand, Nyingmapas usually feel great "trust/faith/devotion" and easily develop pure vision, but on the other hand, they are defeated by desire and attachment, since they have kept in mind that they could have a consort or a partner. When Kagyüpas analyze the life of Marpa, Milarepa and of all these famous great yogis, they say to themselves that the only worthy thing to do is to meditate. Therefore, they rush into their meditation practises, whereas they sometimes lack reliable and stable understanding. For sure, Kagyüpas are very good at meditating, but they are defeated by ignorance since the foundations of their meditation may not be always strong enough. Among the Sakyapas, there are great masters renowned and famous for their deep erudition. Some of them had even had visions of Manjushree. Those following this path are captivated by such masters they assess being much more superior than other masters. But as soon as they have detected a few qualities by other masters, they become jealous. They are charmed by erudition, but defeated by jealousy. Gelugpas do have a great erudition. They take Tsongkhapa as a model. And like their master, they engage themselves in all kind of different debates. They totally focus on philosophical contests and on rhetoric. It seems a bit like pumping up to the extreme the inner tube of a bike's tyre. They are so proud of their debates that they become somehow infatuated. They are involved in passionate arguments, which makes anger grow and grow. They are ready to cut off heads, as a carrot would be cut into slices. Mipam Rinpoche, himself, declared that Nyingmapas teach and claim pure vision, but are defeated by desire and attachment. That Kagyüpas are good at practising, but defeated by mental confusion. That Sakyapas have gained mastery over erudition, but are defeated by jealousy. That Gelugpas are excellent at debating, from which prajna can rise, but are defeated by anger.

While approaching the inner Tantras that require an infinite pure vision, it is critical to eliminate within ourselves, as much as possible, the five conflicting emotions so as to fully experience open-mindedness. It is important to watch to always keep inside the quality of Bodhicitta. There can not be any Vajrayana practise unless there is a genuine true Bodhicitta. Among the general samayas that are linking us to the five Buddhas' families, one of them tells to generate Bodhicitta.

Foreword about the three inner Tantras

The three inner Tantras entail Maha yoga corresponding to the generation stage, Anu yoga corresponding to the dissolution stage and Dzogchen or Ati yoga. Father Tantras refer to Maha yoga comprising eighteen Tantras. Mother Tantras refer to the Anu yoga Tantras. Tantras of enlightened awareness refer to the Tantras in Dzogchen, the Great Perfection. The first six vehicles presented within the ninefold classification going up to Yoga Tantra, have inherited something common to the four great schools of the Tibetan Vajrayana Buddhism. However, when we come to Maha yoga, Anu yoga and Ati yoga (Dzogchen), that is a specific presentation of the Nyingma tradition, the used terminology is different.

Why are Maha, Anu, and Ati yoga unique of the Nyingma tradition? There are some very precise reasons to explain it. Concerning the Kagyü tradition, there are three great scriptures one must know about. Two of the so-called Maitreya Five Treaties, composed by Asanga: "The Supreme Continuity" (Skt. Uttaratantrasastra) and "Clear Distinction between the middle and the extremes" (Skt. Madhyantavibhanga).

In the Nyingma tradition, there are three fundamental scriptures we must know about. It means that we should study them with a master and deepen their profound meaning. They deal with Maha yoga, Anu yoga and Ati yoga.

They entail a root Tantra of Maha yoga (Tib. Do), a root Tantra of Anu yoga (Tib. Gyü) and the indivisible Tantra of Dzogchen. (Tib. Sem Sum). This whole set of Tantras is called "Do Gyü Sem Sum".

In the Sarma tradition, referring to the "recent schools", namely Kagyü, Sakya and Gelug, four empowerments are conferred at the level of the unsurpassable Tantras. Among them, the first three empowerments are openly presented and commented, whereas the fourth one is not. The fourth one is alluded to in "Adamantine words" where the absolute meaning is hidden, but may be perceived by those who have a great insight power.

In the Nyingma so-called "ancient" tradition, the first three empowerments are clearly presented, including the fourth one, which is called "Precious speech empowerment". This fourth empowerment is essential since it introduces to the absolute wisdom. It is clearly detailed. It shows the specificity of this first presentation of the Tantras that were introduced into Tibet in the 8th century and jeopardized in the 9th century while it remained then hidden for a long period of time.

Father Tantras, mother Tantras and non-dual Tantras

We can find father Tantras, mother Tantras and non-dual Tantras. Concerning the male and female Tantras, there is a notion of gender, whereas the non-dual Tantras, which are of higher level, do not convey any idea of gender.

Within the father Tantras the aim is to master the generation stage (Tib. Kyerim) which consists of experiencing oneself as the deity. This practice is shared by all Vajrayana schools.

Within the mother Tantras, it is essential to have our wisdom and enlightened awareness potential burst out and manifest during the dissolution or achievement stage (Tib. Dzogrim). This point is shared by all Vajrayana schools.

Within the non-dual Tantras, the union of Kyerim and Dzogrim is being seeked for. This approach is developed within the three so-called recent schools.

Within the Nyingma tradition the fourth empowerment is introducing the disciple to the nature of mind, namely Rigpa: "The precious speech empowerment", which is the living heart of Dzogchen, during which the master introduces the disciple to primordial wisdom.

Introduction to Rigpa

As it is impossible for the disciple to immediately recognize by himself of by herself this wisdom, the master introduces him or her to the Rigpa while conferring the empowerment of the nature of mind, in order that the disciple can then trace all the way back to the origin, to the ground. Dzogchen clearly and openly explains every required stage to be able to recognize this primordial wisdom and settle in a continuous capacity stream of recognizing it without ever letting it go away. This is very explicitly expounded in a unique way proper to the Nyingmapa tradition.

Before detailing the presentation of each of these three great vehicles that are Maha, Anu and Ati yoga, more general explanations will be given about them.

The foundations of the view within Vajrayana according to the three inner Tantras, Maha, Anu and Ati yoga consist of realizing that all phenomena, every single animated and living creature, which are included in both Samsara and Nirvana- two dimensions otherwise called impure and pure — are part of this indivisibility of both special truths, purity and equanimity.

The wisdom of the five dhyani Buddhas

Within this vision reached out by the yogi in the inner Tantras, — while being helped by the introduction to the nature of mind — the bodies (Skt. Kaya) and wisdom aspects of the five dhyani Buddhas appear. They originally do exist and can be revealed, not by mental fabrication, not by visualization, not by the power of mantras, not even by the power of concentration, but by the combined power of this vision of original purity and equanimity.

The specific feature of these three paths implies that there is no more need to link ourselves to a deity, nor to behave as her or his servant, friend, nor to feel being made out of the same nature, nor to expect to receive any siddhis. What is here prevailing is to strive ourselves to make this wisdom arise, in order that the five dhyani Buddhas can spontaneously manifest.

The proper nature of mind is Enlightenment

The difference between the causal vehicle of characteristic features and the fruition vehicle, namely the vehicle of secret mantras, lies in the fact that within the former one, the proper nature of mind, the mind as it is, is the cause of Enlightenment, whereas within the latter one, the proper nature of mind is Enlightenment, the primordial Buddha, whereby there is no notion of cause.

Liberation within one of the three bardos

Any notion of cause has totally disappeared, but instead remains the purpose of getting to the level of wisdom so as to see that it is simply there. Therefore it is about Great Perfection. On behalf of the power and the sharpness of such a path, there is no doubt that a yogi or yogini can attain Enlightenment in his or her lifetime, or in the bardo of dying thanks to some practices, or at least in the bardo of Dharmata, "the first class bardo". By doing such a practice, it will be impossible not to liberate ourselves at least in the "first class bardo".

Rainbow body: small transfer and great transfer

Within this tradition, realizing Enlightenment means

realizing Enlightenment as "small transfer of rainbow body" and as "great transfer of rainbow body". Enlightenment as "small transfer of rainbow body" has been realized in Tibet by thousands of practitioners. Yet the "great transfer of rainbow body" has not been realized by thousands of people, but as examples, we can mention Vimalamitra, a great Indian master, Guru Rinpoche and many other great Tibetan masters.

Realizing the "great transfer of rainbow body" means that the body itself is taking part into great Enlightenment. It is not a mind that is awakening and whose body is left behind, like a corpse. By following the previous Tantras of Maha yoga, it is impossible in one lifetime or even at the moment of dying or during the bardo of dharmata, to fully awaken by this way.

The perfection of that vision allowing the spontaneous appearing of the original deities makes this path such an extremely fast one. It enables to fully realize Enlightenment at three precise moments: the bardo of this lifetime, the bardo of dying or the bardo of dharmata. Whereas along the other paths, we would have to wait three to sixteen lifetimes, or even more to realize full Enlightenment.

The main point in this foreword about vision within the three inner Tantras is to properly understand what is meant by indivisibility of these two great truths of purity and equanimity that concern all manifested, animated and living phenomena.

Comprising such qualities, the three sets of inner Tantras differ from the outer Tantras through five specific features that justify their superiority over the previous ones.

Five upper features

1. They are vehicles of secret mantras
2. They are vehicles of skilful means
3. They are ajar vehicles
4. They are vehicles dealing with fruition

5. They are vehicles that can be compared to what is incomparable

The terminology specific to secret mantras is likely to be astonishing, but practising is what prevails, because it is the only way to really open up our heart. These five features show that the three sets of inner Tantras are obviously superior to the causal vehicle of characteristic features, but also superior to the three outer Tantras, namely Kriya, Charya and Yoga Tantra.

1. They are vehicles of secret mantras

Meaning of the term "secret mantra" (Tib. Sang Ngag)

We are going to explain the word "secret" (Tib. Sang) whenever used as adjective or noun.

The nature of this profound mandala of the three Kayas, body, speech and immaculate mind of the awakened beings within the three times — past, present and future — do naturally primordially exist. This principle becomes a reality for each sentient being wandering in confusion. The nature of this immaculate body, which is no longer the result of contaminated karma, the nature of the speech endowed with all its qualities as well as the nature of this fully awakened mind, that possesses the two forms of prajna, do primordially exist, but still remain hidden, "secret" to all practitioners, including those, who practise the three outer Tantras.

The reality of a natural primordial Enlightenment can not be grasped by ordinary people, nor by practitioners from Kriya Tantra to Yoga Tantra. Here is the first secret: the reality of Enlightenment is covered or veiled. Therefore, they are mentioned as secret (Tib. Sang) mantras (Tib. Ngag).

The nature of these three principles called stainless body, flawless speech and awakened mind does primordially really exist. But as this truth is beyond the usual understanding, and as it is not presented or compounded to people, who have not had yet any empowerment of any unsurpassable mantra, it is therefore qualified as "secret". This truth is purposely hidden, because it can not be accessible and presented yet.

Mantra (Tib. Ngag)

This is typical within oral tradition and especially during a transmission: giving a word a different meaning than the one we are used to.

Here "mantra" does not mean "mantra" in the usual way, but should rather be understood by the idea of "movement". In the syllable "sang" which means "hidden", there is an idea of a reality of primordial Enlightenment that is hidden to practitioners because they have not attained the necessary level of maturity yet.

The word "mantra" means that the truth of primordial Enlightenment, that had been hidden, can now be clearly expounded. So there is a movement, which enables to switch from a hidden situation to an expounded and accessible one.

The skilful means of these sets of inner Tantras allow to gradually introduce the practitioner to this absolute reality, to make him discover, far beyond the mental level, this reality of primordial Enlightenment. Even if we do experience something else, this reality of primordial Enlightenment has always been totally present.

The expression "secret mantra" is used within the four Vajrayana schools in Tibet.

2. They are vehicles of skilful means

Why do we talk about « skilful means » ?

This impure mind, stained by the notion of "I" also called "yi" (mental), can be presented by the master as being itself part of the primordially enlightened reality. The master must be skilled to get into this so-called impure mind and make the disciple aware of the fact that the stained mind is also taking part into the primordial Enlightenment. It sounds like showing a piece of coal while claiming it is a snowflake. By then, the disciple recognizes the reality. Skilful means are the specificity of this vehicle.

They have got four features: they are supreme, they are many, they are easy and they are fast.

3. They are vajra vehicles

Vajrayana is a vajra vehicle (Skt. Vajra, Tib. Dordje). What does "vajra" mean? The relative truth expounded within the three vehicles, called the cause vehicles, and within the three vehicles of the outer Tantras induces discrimination between phenomena: some have to be rejected, whereas others have to be cultivated. Within Vajrayana, thanks to the fourth empowerment of inner Tantras, we realize that the three doors, our body, speech and mind are the three vajras. Thanks to the power of vision, these body, speech and mind are perceived as being parts of this primordially awakened nature of the stainless body, flawless speech and awakened mind. Through a transmutation process, it is possible to transform from within these three doors into the three vajras.

Affixing the three seals

Thanks to the empowerment, enhanced by a sustained practice carried out by the practitioner, the master can affix on the ordinary body (Tib. Lü) of the disciple the seal of the stainless Body (Tib. Ku). In Tibetan, "Ku" is the honorific form of the word "Lü". The master affixes on the ordinary speech of the disciple the seal of the stainless Speech. On the ordinary intellect of the disciple, the master affixes the seal of the awakened Mind. "Affixing the seal" means that it is possible to transmute from within these three principles that are experienced in an ordinary way and turn them into three enlightened principles through a kind of alchemical process.

Here is a short example: during a meditation session, as far as the body is concerned, we spontaneously become Vajrasattva. The seal of the stainless body of the deity is affixed on our ordinary body. While we are repeating the mantra, the long or the short one, the seal of the stainless speech of the deity is affixed on the ordinary speech. On the ordinary mental is the seal of the self-discriminating wisdom

ourselves as the deity confers liberation by meditating upon two special truths: the special absolute and relative truths. The special relative truth is great purity and the special absolute truth is great equanimity. As a result, Maha yoga consists of meditating upon this indivisibility, that is to say meditating ourselves and our primordially pure mind as appearing as the deity. Being "linked to the absolute truth" means being at the very heart of the great equanimity. Visualizing ourselves as the deity is the great purity. Both truths are inseparable. The deity can not appear if the vision is not here, if we are not connected to this great inner state of equanimity. Such a practice is conferring liberation.

Etymology

Maha yoga means "great yoga".

The six linking points

1. Entrance's door(Tib. Jugo)

The entrance's door entails four empowerments of unsurpassable Tantras.

1. Vase empowerment

2. Secret empowerment

3. Empowerment of awakened awareness/wisdom

4. Speech empowerment

This is being explained in the King Tantra, namely the Guru Yoga Tantra.

1. Vase empowerment

The vase empowerment entails ten blessing empowerments and five power empowerments.

a) Ten blessing empowerments

At the outer level, there are five crown empowerments and five silk cap empowerments.

b) Five power empowerments

At the inner level, there are five power empowerments.

2. Secret empowerment

Three profound secret empowerments.

3. Empowerment of awakened wisdom/awareness

4. Speech empowerment

The precious speech empowerment is an introduction to Rigpa, the self-discriminating wisdom.

2. View (Tib. Tava)

Sevenfold cycle of the absolute

The view is entailed within the sevenfold cycle of absolute and within the special relative truth. It is a special codified language belonging to the ancient tradition. It means that the absolute possesses seven aspects. The first aspect is Dhatu, the very absolute. The second one is wisdom. The absolute can not exist without wisdom. The five other aspects are the stainless body, the flawless speech, the awakened mind, the qualities and the four forms of Enlightenment activities, such as pacification, subjugation, prosperity and growth, and destruction. These seven aspects are called the sevenfold cycle of the absolute.

One should always keep in mind both aspects: wisdom of the absolute and the corresponding manifestation, which is appearing through the features of the deity. From this sevenfold cycle of the absolute, a reality is thrilling with power, radiance and dynamism. It means that there is a kind of springing, a luminosity that is shown off and outwardly directed. From that point, the five aggregates (Sk Skandha), the six elements, the six seats (the five sensorial organs and the mental organ) are experienced by the yogi or the yogini as being part of the bodies of the five dhyani Buddhas.

Even if the practitioner gets involved later on in the realization process of a specific yidam, this yidam will always be associated to one of the five dhyani Buddhas. These five dhyani Buddhas are one manifestation of the five fundamental wisdoms. What does this special relative truth mean? It means that the yogi or yogini experiences skandhas, elements, sensorial organs and mental organ as being body

The twenty-five secondary samayas of the ancient schools are not listed here.

4. Meditation (Tib. Gompa)

Meditation consists of practising Kyerim, the generation stage as well as Dzogrim, the dissolution or achievement stage. There are four ways for meditating the generation stage. It is possible to meditate Kyerim from the birth occurring through a womb, from an egg, in mould or from an instant birth. Kyerim from the birth through a womb and from an egg are the two most practised forms of Kyerim. These forms of Kyerim must be practised, as the Tibetan expression tells within "the framework of the three forms of concentration".

5. Conduct (Tib. Chödpa)

There are three forms of action:

1. With development;

2. Without development;

3. Neither with, nor without development.

6. Result (Tib. Drebu)

There are four maturing stages: four Vidyadharas.

Here, Vidyadhara refers to realization and not to an individual.

1. Maturing Vidyadhara

2. Vidyadhara of power over life or immortality.

3. Vidyadhara of Mahamudra.

4. Vidyadhara of spontaneous presence.

Thanks to such practices, practitioners who are endowed with:

1. Upper faculties can attain Enlightenment in their present lifetime.

2. Medium faculties can attain Enlightenment in the bardo at the moment of dying.

3. Lower faculties can attain Enlightenment in the first class bardo of dharmata.

Breaking out the stream of Samsara

Practices of Maha yoga deal above all with Kyerim, namely the generation stage. The essential function of Kyerim is to delete all traces and imprints, that are dragging us into birth, according to the four modes of birth: womb, egg, mould and instant birth. As long as we have not purified all these imprints corresponding to the four modes of birth, it is impossible to break the stream of Samsara. The subtlest imprints, namely those from the three visions transfer (cf. page 16), are linked to our parents gametes. These gametes are the origin of our body formation, associated with the wind element that is the support of our mind. The wind is made out of this inseparable union of subtle mind and subtle wind, what is called the consciousness of the being within bardo, that will join the egg and the gametes during fertilization. The consciousness, that has gone through the bardo, carries with it all traces that have been accumulated births after births. If we do not care to practice Maha yoga to purify these imprints, it will not be possible to get out of Samsara. From the inner Tantras point of view, these imprints related to the three transfer visions are the subtlest one that should necessarily be removed and purified in order to stop the samsaric circle. As it is within Sutrayana, the causal vehicle of characteristic features, the cause of births is ignorance, the first of the twelve interdependent links. Within the three inner Tantras, the true cause of being dragged into birth is the imprints of the three transfer visions: clarity, reddish vision and pitch-black darkness that occur at the very moment, whereby one leaves his or her body and enters into the bardo.

Gametes, winds and consciousness

When the ovule is being fertilized by the spermatozoid in the uterus of the future mother, at this very moment conception is happening. These gametes are immediately joined by a consciousness that has been carried by wind and

Anu yoga, the path that follows the path of the great union

Before starting listening to the teaching, it is important to be in the right motivation.

Being in the pure vision of Vajrayana is the ground for our listening to the teachings.

Within Vajrayana, two types of motivation are required.

The ground motivation requires to look upon all beings of the six levels of existence with great compassion since all of them have been our mothers and fathers in our numerous previous lives. It is not possible to feel unconcerned by the fate of beings. Moved by their suffering, in whatever degree or level it might be because of their ignorance, we give rise within ourselves to a strong determination to realize full Enlightenment, so that we will be able to lead them to the pristine land of Samantabhadra. This motivation is based on vast and generous thoughts.

Then, we have the specific motivation of Vajrayana, which is pure vision.

As we can not access to Vajrayana unless we have received the liberating empowerments and corresponding commentaries, all our visual perceptions are associated to the unstained body (Skt. Nirmanakaya, Tib. Tulku) of the deity, the lama and the lineage masters. All our auditive perceptions merge in our practice with the flawless speech of the deity, the lama and the lineage masters. All our thoughts are united to the wisdom of the deity, the lineage masters and the lama, who had conferred us the empowerment. By this way, we can experience all fields of perceptions — visual, auditive and cognitive — that arise during the post-meditation phase as a manifestation of the great primordial wisdom. This is the right motivation within Vajrayana. We are hoisting into the level of that limitless pure vision. Once we are well rooted in this kind of motivation, we can then properly pay attention to what is going to be taught.

The foundation of Hinayana is renouncement. But it is also the common base to all Buddhadharma practitioners, in other words the Buddha's teachings. Any single progress on our path is impossible, unless we keep present in our mind this idea of renouncement.

The springforce within Mahayana is love and compassion.

Yet, the major point within Vajrayana deals with samaya, but beforehand, it is necessary to develop trust and respect. This attitude based on trust and open-mindedness can only be experienced, once we have transcended the mental and thus, we are within our true profound nature. Next, we must develop love and compassion. Once we have received an empowerment, we commit ourselves to uphold samayas, which require to develop pure vision.

This pure vision enables us to experience that all possible manifested and living phenomena are deprived of any self-existence and are simply part of this limitless purity. It is non-created and therefore it is primordially pure. Experiencing it is the base samaya within Vajrayana. It is the keystone of this palace, whose entrance door is the empowerment.

It is difficult to straightforwardly experience it. But at the beginning, through the power of the empowerment, of the trust/faith, it is possible to feel or to hint at what is the truth. Thanks to the empowerment, we can begin to get familiar with pure vision. The outlines gradually appear and then get more and more precise.

Within Vajrayana, whatever school we are connected to, as well as within the Nyingmapa tradition, at the end of the

Etymology

In sanskrit, "Anu" means "being close". The point of awakened awareness is above all the critical aspect within this path, is an account for the designation of "close yoga".

The six linking points

1.Entrance's door(Tib. Jugo)

As it is within Maha yoga, there are also here four empowerments:

1. Vase empowerment
2. Secret empowerment
3. Awakened awareness empowerment
4. Precious speech empowerment

It would take too long to detail these four empowerments, but I am going to give you a kind of summary, that will help you get the main inner meaning and essential power.

1. Vase empowerment

Vase empowerment aims at discarding veils that have been accumulated because of a distorted use of our body, and at fertilizing within ourselves the seeds, so that, in the future, we will be able to fully realize Nirmanakaya: a manifested body whose function will be to serve all sentient beings.

Why do we talk about vase empowerment? Before conferring the empowerment, the master, through the power of his concentration, visualises the vase, on a very subtle level, as being the palace of the deities' Mandela. This vase must be experienced by the disciples, who are going to receive the empowerment, as being the palace of the deity. The ambrosia water or nectar, which is contained in the vase, is visualised by the master as being the deity Mandela. The vase and its nectar are used as a support for the representation and for the realization of the deity palace with the deities Mandela.

The master puts the vase on the head of everyone to symbolize the function of this first empowerment, namely discarding all veils related to a mistaken body use and fertilizing the seeds that will enable to realize Nirmanakaya. Each empowerment aims at purifying body, speech and mind. Yet, the essential function is to purify the body veils, in order to realize all possible forms of manifestations, all Nirmanakayas to serve all beings.

2. Secret empowerment

The essential function of the secret empowerment is to discard the veils, which have been accumulated because of a distorted speech use, and to fertilize the seeds that will enable the disciple to realize all different aspects of Sambhogakaya.

Until Atisha came to Tibet in the 9th century, this empowerment was not symbolically, but instead really conferred. However, the glorious Atisha brought a few changes, so that this empowerment has no longer been conferred the way it had been done before. Using some cinabre powder (Skt. Sindura, Tib. Li-khri) something is drawn on a mirror and the master touches our throat with his/her ring-finger. Although the empowerment is symbolic, the transmission is actually genuine. This is the new way of confering this empowerment, from which we receive all blessings and spiritual grace.

The genuine secret empowerment

What was the former genuine secret empowerment like? As long as we have a limitless and total trust in Vajrayana, the master can use many different means, according to his or her assessment, in order to lead the disciple to the recognition of the state of primordial wisdom. In ancient times, the guru, who was conferring the empowerment, was a fully awakened master. For each empowerment, he had only one or two disciples at the same time, whose trust was perfectly unwavering. This guru had a spiritual consort, with whom he was practising sexual Tantra. The empowerment consisted of transmitting on the tongue of his favoured disciples the vital essences resulting from his experience of blissfulness, in order to bring them to directly recognize Rigpa.

This empowerment was only conferred to the most advanced disciples. Nowadays, empowerments are conferred to everyone in general. The empowerment introducing to Rigpa, as it is conferred today, certainly enables to recognize wisdom, but we may however wonder, whether all necessary conditions are really gathered to make this recognition possible. As far as the genuine secret empowerment is concerned, as the guru used to confer it in ancient times, by putting his vital essences on the disciple's tongue, the required conditions were then all present to enable the disciple to successfully recognize Rigpa.

When he came to Tibet, Atisha, though he was not prudish than anyone else, estimated that this kind of empowerment was not appropriate any longer to the present times. While the five forms of wanes were spreading, such practices might have been grasped through the prism of an impure mind, thus giving rise to distorted views (Tib. Logpar), and hence creating a very serious karma since it would spoil what is most sacred. Therefore, this practice has been conferred in its symbolic aspect. A realized master must have a tantric consort, but his mind has to be really mature enough.

One aphorism tells: « An ordinary being can not prejudge the deeds of the master ». The history of Tibet is full of these kinds of accounts of masters, whose behaviour might somehow have puzzled the audience. Some of them, with wife and children, constantly thirsty, always a jug of alcohol kept at hand, were not at all matching with the traditional image of an Indian ascete eating very little.

A dog can not judge a lion

Another saying tells « a dog can not judge a lion ». A lion is absolutely majestic compared to a dog. A dog perfectly knows that a lion is majestic, but while wondering about it, the dog has already been eaten up by the lion. The morality of this story is that we'd rather look at our own mind and check, where exactly we are up to, before judging our master or other people.

The one who used to drink tchang

A story is frequently reported in Southern Tibet telling that when Guru Rinpoche arrived in these very remote regions, people noticed that he was drinking a lot of tchang, which is a kind of Tibetan beer. Then they started to drink like the master, thinking that « if this is good for him, it will be good for us ». As a result they were found drunk. Then, Guru Rinpoche asked them what they were doing. They answered that they were just following his example. At this very moment, Guru Rinpoche let the tchang he had drunk get out from each of his fingers and told them that once they would be able to do alike, they would be allowed to drink some tchang !

When Milarepa met Marpa

When Milarepa met for the first time Marpa, the great translator, whose incomparable disciple he was to become, he was somehow puzzled. Before he got to know him, Milarepa had imagined his master in a certain way. He imagined him indeed as being « a great yogi totally absorbed in meditation». But Marpa was a lay-man, and he also did appreciate drinking some tchang too.

First Milarepa found Dakmema, Marpa's wife. With great respect, Milarepa told her that he would like to meet Marpa, the master. Dakmema answered him that Marpa was at the fields. Puzzled, Milarepa was wondering how it would be possible that the master could be at the fields, and what he would be doing there. Would he grow corns? Would he plough his fields with ox? So, Milarepa went to the fields and Marpa, thanks to his clear-sightedness abilities could see Milarepa arriving. Milarepa talked to the master with great respect: « I am coming to meet the great master Marpa». Marpa replied: « Go away, beggar! Buzz off! Can't you see that I am busy now working in the fields! » Marpa was angry since he had perceived that Milarepa was not entirely trusting him, there were still some doubts. Therefore it was first of all necessary to purify his lack of trust.

Do Khyentse Yeshe, the crazy wisdom

As a great master endowed with profound knowledge as well as picturesque and colourful character, Do Khyentse Yeshe lived in Eastern Tibet. Like many people who were moving a lot, he was carrying his scriptures on wooden supports, inside his clothes, one hanging on his chest and the other one on his back, all tied up with a large belt. Some people were astonished to see him travelling packed up this way and asked him why he was travelling like that. Do Khyentse Yeshe, who was a very great scholar, used to reply in a tone filled with crazy wisdom: « Don't you know that my whole body of flesh and blood has turned into the word of Buddha? ». People were puzzled and, some of them, among Gelugpas, used to call him "the wrong Nyingmapa", for he had very disconcerting words and thus he was destabilizing people. Some even insulted him considering he was totally mad.

One day, while he was at the village main square, holding a dagger at his belt, as men usually were wearing one in Eastern Tibet, he caught two dogs, one white and the other black that he cut in their middle and whose different halves he joined together: the black half with the white one, and so implanting the head of the white dog with the back of the black one and vice versa. And the dogs, without noticing anything, kept on moving along! This can illustrate the following aphorism: «Ordinary human beings ought not prejudge the deeds of the master».

In ancient times, a master, in union with his spiritual consort, who was herself a wisdom emanation, was conferring empowerments to a few mature disciples: it is actually difficult to make ourselves an idea of what this kind of similar deeds really imply. But do not imagine that they are porn movie alike!

Dilgo Khyentse Rinpoche

The Dzogchen master of His Holiness the Dalaï Lama was His Holiness Dilgo Khyentse Rinpoche. Dilgo Khyentse Rinpoche went plenty of times to Dharamsala, to the private palace of His Holiness the Dalaï Lama, to confer him empowerments and teachings. When Dilgo Khyentse Rinpoche was conferring His Holiness the Dalaï Lama the teaching on the Guhyagarbhatantra, it gave rise to many commentaries. One day, a member of the government in exile started talking about this kind of subject with some other persons. Some of them, on ground of their pure vision, said: « A tantric practitioner like Dilgo Khyentse Rinpoche is fantastic! » Someone else, who had a less pure vision said: « Well, fine, he has got a wife, so do I. He feels desire, so do I. So what makes the difference between both of us?». Obviously, the latter one had not the capacity to get a true understanding.

This is the reason why, even today, when receiving the second empowerment, as a symbol of the ancient traditional way, the nectar mixed with honey is put on the disciple tongue.

This empowerment aims at purifying the veils which have been accumulated by a wrong and distorted use of speech, and thus fertilizing the seeds that will enable us to fully awaken to the Dharmakaya dimension and to realize different forms of Sambhogakaya manifestations.

A spot of red paste on the throat of the disciple

During some empowerments, the nectar is not seen but the master merely touches the mirror with the red paste and puts a spot of red paste on the throat of the disciple. However, the symbolic strength of the empowerment is alike. It could seem to be funny stories, but when we come to Vajrayana, we get to another dimension.

An ordinary mind with an ordinary mental could be likely to condemn and judge these different deeds, but when we come to this kind of dimension, ordinary mental is useless. It can no longer be accurately operating. It does not suit any longer to this reality. These anecdotes are used to show the discrepancy between these both levels of perception.

3. Awakened awareness empowerment

The awakened awareness empowerment aims at discarding the veils which have been accumulated through a distorted use of our mind, and thus at fertilizing the seeds that will enable us to realize Dharmakaya, the state of perfectly awakened mind. When this third empowerment is conferred, crystal is used as a support. It does not symbolize the consciousness considered as mental, but rather the mind in its absolutely empty nature, for, mind is not self-existing and is not like an entity. Some exercises mean to help us be aware that mind has no reality that could be called mind, even if at the same time on the relative level, we are able of thinking and perceiving. But as far as this empowerment is concerned, it is much subtler, more profound. As a matter of fact, mind is space-like limitless and uncreated, and yet just like in a crystal mirror, reflections can appear. From this totally vast and pristine dimension of mind, anything can appear. The support given to represent mind is crystal. The used metaphor is "like a rainbow in the sky". Sky is absolutely vast and pristine. From this uncreated state occurs a manifesting power. In Tibetan it is referred to as "the colours of a rainbow" to show both its unfolding aspect as well as its colourful aspect. This rainbow has non-self-existence. It is void though it is manifesting. As it is manifesting, its essence is uncreated.

4. Precious speech empowerment

The fourth empowerment, the precious speech empowerment, aims at simultaneously discarding the accumulated veils of a distorted use of our three doors: body, speech and mind. The master fertilizes the seeds that will enable the disciple to realize the three kayas. In this tradition, the fourth empowerment is introducing to Rigpa, to the primordial knowledge that is the very foundation of the whole practice of Dzogchen.

Practising Dzogchen is impossible if you have not first recognized and acknowledged Rigpa. The fourth empowerment is introducing us to this reality called Rigpa. Nowadays, when it comes to this empowerment, the master may lead the disciple to it in a bias way. However, the true fourth empowerment is indeed a direct introduction to Rigpa, to a dimension in which practising Dzogchen becomes possible. It can not occur before. One can be introduced to Rigpa through examples or in a direct manner.

Being introduced to Rigpa through examples

When the master is conferring the Nyingthik Yashi empowerment, one of the great commentaries by Longtchenpa on Dzogchen practice, he may tell his disciple: «Now fly off to the Eastern direction, thousands of kilometres far from here to reach such pure land! Fly like a bird or leap like a tiger, and when you are about to fly or to leap, watch your mind! Watch what your mind is!»? Obviously, there is nothing to be seen! At this very moment, the disciple can recognize this reality, called Rigpa, uncreated and yet perfectly knowing/discriminating. In this case, it is an introduction to Rigpa through examples.

This empowerment aims at discarding the veils that have been accumulated by a wrong and distorted use of our three doors and also at fertilizing the seeds that will enable us to realize the three kayas. As far as the three inner Tantras, Maha, Anu and Ati yoga are concerned, the entrance's doorwill always be the same, namely the four empowerments from vase to speech. But considering the topic on a deeper level, as it is immense and vast, there are actually thirty-six empowerments.

Thirty-six empowerments within Anu yoga

- ten empowerments on outer level,
- eleven empowerments on inner level,
- thirteen empowerments dealing with practice and realization,
- two secret empowerments.

2. View (Tib. Tava)

The three mandalas: father, mother and son

Regarding the view, the purpose is to achieve a kind of realization dealing with the nature of the three Mandala: the father Mandela of Samantabhadra, the mother mandala of Samantabhadri and the son mandala that is Blissfulness.

The Samantabhadri mandala or Dhatu

What does the Samantabhadri mandala refer to? Samantabhadri is not a person. The Samantabhadri mandala is the wisdom that realizes that all possible manifested and living phenomena are part of Dhatu, namely absolute emptiness. The word "object" (Tib. Yül) is very important since it encompasses all manifested and living phenomena.

The Samantabhadra mandala or Yeshe

What does the Samantabhadra mandala refer to ? It means gaining a direct understanding of "the self-existing wisdom". It is primordial. It does not depend on any cause and condition. Attaining this reality that is called primordially pure mind, that has never been contaminated, is the mandala of Samantabhadra (Tib. Küntuzangpo).

The son mandala or the Bodhicitta mandala

For that yogini, the mandala of the absolute Bodhicitta consists of understanding that Dhatu, which is symbolized by Samantabhadri, and Yeshe, which is symbolized by Samantabhadra are indivisible. There is no absolute that would be an object known by wisdom. There is just this absolute reality that is self-knowing, self-discriminating since it knows itself. When the practitioner is experiencing this indivisibility, he or she is accessing to the son mandala of blissfulness, which is also called the Bodhicitta mandala. Why is it called "son"? Because Samantabhadra is symbolized by the father and Samantabhadri by the mother: it symbolizes a reality that is beyond our ordinary mental.

3. Ethic (Tib. Tsültrim)

Ethic based on two samayas

The ethic consists of upholding a root samaya and a branch samaya, both of them enable us to become "master of the base". It means to be bound by the three doors and having full control upon body, speech and mind. Being bound to get the mastery. This is a nice way to picture it. Imagine plenty of grass blades scattered all about and once tied up we make a great bunch out of them, a lovely bouquet. The three scattering doors can be tied up by samayas.

Ethic in nine root samayas

Within the first root samaya there are four samayas of certainty.

Within the second root samaya there are twenty-eight ordinary samayas.

Within the third root samaya there are four special samayas.

Within the fourth root samaya there are twenty-three samayas related to yogi practices.

Within the fifth root samaya there are twenty samayas related to practice dealing with realization.

Within the sixth root samaya there are four samayas related to our daily behaviour.

Within the seventh root samaya there are samayas related to abandoning the five times.

Within the eighth root samaya there are samayas related to deleting the four extremes: existence, non-existence, both of them or none of them.

Within the ninth root samaya there are samayas related to the view. And so forth, altogether it makes around one hundred of samayas. Through upholding the nine root samayas, the secondary ones will be consequently upheld.

Actually, when reducing all of them to the innermost essence, there are two major samayas left. Which are they?

The samaya without upholding and the samaya with upholding

When we are in the meditation phase, we are in the samaya without upholding. We are in the heart of the absolute. We are beyond any idea of samaya to be upheld. We are within unity.

When we are in the post-meditation phase, we find ourselves in the samaya with upholding, it means that among all samayas that have to be upheld, there is only one we have to constantly uphold, we are bound to: we ought to always be moved by love and compassion. If we are not living as a being of complete generosity, limitless love and compassion for all beings, then, we have lost all other samayas.

To put it in a nusthell, all samayas can be reduced into two major ones : the samaya without upholding, namely being at the heart of the absolute and the samaya with upholding, namely making sure that we are always in a wholehearted generosity driven by love and compassion.

4. Meditation. (Tib. Gompa)

The purpose is to get to the meaning of the reality, to reach out this reality, whereby there is no thought. Here, the mental is not working anymore, it has stopped. By this way it is possible to perceive emptiness.

"Getting to the letter" comprises two paths:

1. The liberation path

2. The path of skilful means

1. The liberation path

The liberation path consists of practising Kyerim which means in a first step generating the deity, and then keeping up the mental clarity of the deity, and thus we will be able to recite the corresponding mantra.

2. The path of skilful means

Skilful means enable us to work on "upper doors" and on "lower doors".

a) Working on "upper doors"

It deals with practices on channels (Skt. Nadi, Tib. Tsa), wind energies (Skt. Vayu, Tib. Lung) and vital essences (Skt. Bindu, Tib. Tigle). We ought first to meditate on winds, then on channels before starting the different yogic exercises. By gaining flexibility within the subtle body, we get a way to recognize Rigpa. It is not a direct way but instead we use skillful means.

b) Working on "lower doors"

Once they have worked on upper doors, yogis have achieved the required mature level that will enable them to practise union through the practice of Tumo. Regarding men, they can rely on their spiritual consort and practise coupling to experience blissfulness within the three realms. From this experience of blissfulness, both partners can come to a direct recognition of Riga. It is all about getting to recognize the nature of this experience of pleasure gained by blissfulness, the very wisdom of blissfulness.

5. Conduct (Tib. Chödpa)

We have attained here a very advanced level of practice. The aim is to understand that every thing that is part of the reality — may it be any object that is grasped or any consciousness as subject that is grasping, namely the traditional pattern subject-object – is the result of blissfulness interplay. In essence there is merely this experience of blissfulness. Once the yogi has understood that every single thing is part of this blissfulness interplay, through his behaviour he can transcend the idea of anything to be cultivated or to be abandoned. Every aspect of his behaviour is right since he experiences it within that blissfulness. We are here at the very heart of Vajrayana, which means experiencing great purity and great equanimity, while being aware that we must first understand great purity before achieving great equanimity. Acknowledging the absolute enables us to perceive the whole phenomena as being a pure manifestation of deities. A practitioner with such a view can more sharply perceive (and even with his or her body, since he or she practises Anu yoga and thus works on lower and upper doors) this notion of something good or bad, that has to be abandoned or cultivated. He or she is transcending these notions as such a practitioner is at the heart of equanimity whereby everything has got a unique taste.

6. Result (Tib. Drebu)

A practitioner, who is at the very heart of this view, meditation and behaviour, can within one lifetime fully realize the twenty-five aspects of fruition.

What are these twenty-five aspects ? The five ground aspects that are 1) unstained body, 2) immaculate speech, 3) awakened mind, 4) qualities (Tib. Yö nten) and 5) four Enlightened activities (Tib. Trinle). Each of them entails five sides. By practising Anu yoga, these twenty-five aspects of fruition can be realized within one single lifetime.

Dzogchen, the path of Great Perfection

When we are about listening to teachings or about practising, it is very important to be in the right state of mind and generate the proper motivation. Above all it deals with looking upon all sentient beings of the six realms with love and compassion since, at a given time; they all have been our mothers and fathers in our numerous previous lives. When we do so, we eventually become aware that their fate is actually, by one way or another, constantly doomed to suffering, whatever form it takes. Hence, we feel very concerned, to such an extent that we experience indeed a kind of profound connection that is linking us to all beings. It gives therefore rise to great compassion towards beings and thus, we develop a strong determination to attain Enlightenment for their sake in order to set them in the "primordial state of the protector", that is Samantabhadra, pure prajna. This is how the first type of motivation related to space-like thinking and the second one related to great diversity of skillful means to be put into force, are generated. This richness results from the understanding that all possible manifested and living phenomena are part of the great emptiness and that Nirvana as well as Samsara belong to the Great Purity Equanimity, a totally uncreated dimension from which great purity and unfolding of deities appear.

The quintessence of all the teachings Buddha gave during fifty years, its remarkable richness, these many various paths he offered to all his different disciples, are collected, according to the Nyingmapa tradition, in the nine progressive vehicles.

The nine progressive yana are classified into three great vehicles. The "rising vehicle through unfolding" entails Sutras. The "knowledge vehicle through asceticism" entails the three outer Tantras. And for practitioners endowed with the finest upper faculties, granted with unshakeable trust and pure vision, the "vehicle of transcending skilful means" entails the three inner Tantras.

The three inner Tantras are also subdivided into three: Maha yoga is meant for upper disciples endowed with lower faculties, Anu yoga is meant for upper disciples endowed with medium faculties, Ati yoga or Dzogchen is meant for upper disciples endowed with superior faculties. Maha yoga gives the keys to understand the ground of all phenomena. Anu yoga — and it is indeed explained in one of the Tantras — must be considered as the path for all phenomena. Ati yoga or Dzogchen introduces to the fruit of all phenomena and allows to reach out to the ultimate vision of reality.

Maha yoga, also called "Maha yoga of generation", emphasizes on Kyerim, the generation stage of the deity and on skillful means. Anu yoga stresses the aspect of awakened awareness and Dzogrim, the dissolution stage. Ati yoga or Dzogchen insists on the union of both aspects: generation and dissolution, Kyerim and Dzogrim.

Clear Light

Within practice, the workground of Dzogchen is Clear Light, Rigpa, awakened awareness.

Dzogchen, the non-dual Tantra

Maha yoga focuses on skilful means. Therefore the eighteen Tantras within Maha yoga are designated as "father Tantra". Anu yoga focuses on awakened awareness, wisdom. Therefore it is designated as "mother Tantra".

Dzogchen encompasses a set of Tantras designated as non-dual since they are neither "mother" nor "father". It is beyond this classification. Therefore it is designated as "non-dual Tantra".

Dzogchen entails a set of Tantras called "non-dual Tantras". Within Dzogchen, the true knowledge/awareness is perceived, without union nor separation from Rigpa. Once engaged into Dzogchen, we ought to always keep this view of Rigpa in mind.

Maha yoga is intended for people, whose dominant defilement is anger-aggression. Anu yoga is intended for people, whose dominant defilement is desire-attachment. Ati yoga or Dzogchen is intended for people, whose dominant defilement is ignorance.

It may sound rather contradictory. On one hand, Dzogchen is meant for disciples endowed with superior upper faculties, and on the other hand it is also meant for practitioners whose major defilement is ignorance.

The three characteristics of Dzogchen

1. First characteristic

Dzogchen has got a primordially awakened nature. This is the cornerstone. If we do not consider that this nature, which is Buddha nature, is primordially awakened, we will obviously miss the point.

2. Second characteristic

Dzogchen is a skilful means that enables to free ourselves on the very ground of Rigpa, which is a dimension of consciousness that is awakening to its true nature. The rising "Rigpa" must merely keep on growing to make liberation come true.

3. Third characteristic

Dzogchen is deprived of notions related neither to goodness or badness, nor to anything needed to be cultivated or abandoned, nor to hope or fear. Being within Dzogchen, means being in the heart of the view, in this awareness that enables us to overcome this duality.

These three characteristics help, even if it is rather theoretical, defining the essence of the word Dzogchen.

Among the nine yana of the Nyingmapa tradition, Dzogchen is the peak, the absolute Tantra. It is defined as "absolute fruition" or "spreading wisdom that is all pervading", or "origin of wisdom", or else "the base from which wisdom can radiate".

A great Pandita stated that Dzogchen should be understood as the very manifestation of wisdom. It is like the supreme Vajradhara, the unique lord that encompasses everyone and everything as Dzogchen can merely be understood in this wisdom dimension. Dzogchen enables us to gradually experience the very heart of this wisdom dimension.

Etymology

"Ati yoga" means "supreme yoga". Dzogchen is the absolute or supreme yoga, for it is beyond duality. Maha yoga is the yoga of skilful means, whereas Anu yoga is the yoga of awakened awareness.

The six linking points

1. Entrance's door (Tib. Jugo)

Dzogchen is composed of three great types of practices. All of them are based on a presentation of Rigpa.

1. At the outer level, Semde or "the different types of consciousness" insists on the clarity of Rigpa.

2. At the inner level, Longde or "the different types of space" focuses on the emptiness of consciousness compared to limitless space.

3. At the secret level, Men Ngak or "the different types of precepts" confers key instructions that will enable us to remain in the view.

These three great types of practices will be developed later on.

Similarly to the previous Tantras, four empowerments are the gateway into Dzogchen, but the most important one is the fourth empowerment, which is the precious speech empowerment.

The precious speech empowerment

The fourth "precious speech empowerment" entails four empowerments:

1. Empowerment with support.

2. Empowerment without development.

3. Empowerment without any single development.

4. Ultimately direct empowerment without any development at all.

The goal of these four empowerments is to discard:

1. the body veils,

2. the speech veils,

3. the mind veils,

4. the finest veils that obscure what can be known and the capacity of directly knowing all phenomena also called omniscience. These finest veils are like the traces left back by the first three types of veils of body, speech and mind.

These four empowerments allow the disciple to do some specific practices.

What are they?

1. The first empowerment allows the disciple to practise Kyerim within Maha yoga.

2. The second empowerment allows the disciple to practise "Tumo" and while practising being able to reach out the wisdom of Bliss-Emptiness.

3. The third empowerment allows the disciple to realize the wisdom of primordial purity. As one of the greatest aspects within Dzogchen relies on spontaneous presence and primordial purity, this empowerment enables the disciple to penetrate this wisdom.

4. The fourth empowerment allows the disciple to directly realize the spontaneous presence. It does not deal here with mental representation, nor visualization, but rather with sensitive experiences, namely getting vision of deities.

As it has just been shown, the true entrance's door into practising Dzogchen, within both aspects of primordial purity and spontaneous presence, is the precious speech empowerment. This empowerment inspires profound respect since it introduces disciples to the very essence of Dzogchen. The first three empowerments have not revealed the absolute reality yet, whereas the fourth one explicitly shows what Rigpa is, that is to say the absolute reality.

Only Dzogchen shows in a detailed way all multiple aspects of this absolute reality and how to explore it.

A crystal-like reality

Every way of approaching Anu yoga, Maha yoga and the other previous vehicles as well as other Vajrayana methods, is related to the empowerment of awakened awareness or wisdom. The third empowerment is a symbolical one, also called empowerment through example. For, the purpose is to bring the disciple to experiencing as much as possible through channels, winds and the practice of Tumo as well as recognizing wisdom, joy of bliss, and so forth.... Within the Nyingmapa tradition, this empowerment is conferred through showing a crystal. Crystal symbolically represents the nature of mind. It is merely a piece of crystal, but if a single light ray touches it, it is then enough to have colours appear. This is the whole point. Linked to this uncreated dimension, there is a dynamic power that makes the five wisdoms unfold as five colored lights, like a rainbow in the sky.

« This is the way it is for the fourth empowerment! »

Once we have come to the third empowerment, the master shows the disciple a piece of crystal and says: «This is the way it is for the fourth empowerment»! It depends then on the disciple, according to his faculties, to get the vajra words of the master who remains somehow mysterious. Rigpa is not explicitly introduced.

2. View (Tib. Tava)

What is the view like within Dzogchen? It is necessary to see that all possible manifested and living phenomena are in a state of primordial Awakening, without any single effort.

What do they awaken « in » and « to »?

All possible manifested and living phenomena have got an awakened nature "within" the essence of great wisdom. The path leads to awakening "to" this great wisdom.

Phenomena are primordially in an awakened state without any single effort, within the essence of great wisdom that is self-existing and called Dharmakaya. The view in Dzogchen, to which the practitioner is introduced to, even if he or she perceives it only a few seconds, is that state, whereby everything is completude.

What is the state of completude like?

Great Perfection

Another fundamental aspect is also called Great Perfection. All possible phenomena are part of the same essence, namely Great Perfection or primordial unique great wisdom: Dharmakaya.

Beseeching the three kayas

Here are two verses of a prayer recited in some Dzogchen practices, "beseeching the three kayas": they give a rather good idea of what is Dzogchen.

The first two verses show the kind of relationship we ought to have towards the three times:

1. No searching in the past;

2. No anticipating the future;

3. No manipulating the present time.

There are some techniques designed to gain this mastery. Their purpose is to enable the movement of our thoughts to settle down without interfering, while being able to get out of our usual pattern of the three times. When we learn not to interfere, and when we know how to stay in this dimension of awareness, the movement of our thoughts is absorbing, and even if it occurs, thoughts can be recognized in their absolute nature, namely the essence of wisdom. Thoughts arise and then disappear.

Mental liberation

Recognizing that thoughts are part of this primordial wisdom allow our thoughts to be freed within the base of Rigpa, within Dharmakaya. Thoughts, being neither rejected nor accepted, are somehow transmuted. They are liberated into Dharmakaya, the wisdom state.

This topic requires much more instructions for practising. Here are just a few hints, yet the above mentioned verses can give us a good idea of what the path is like.

The innermost essence of Dzogchen is recognizing that all phenomena are primordially awakened. The view in Dzogchen consists of not considering phenomena with an impure mind, but instead regarding them in an absolute manner, through another viewpoint, naturally keeping in mind that all possible phenomena are part of Rigpa. They are primordially in an awakened state.

The magic of recognizing Enlightenment or not

Claiming that we are all Buddhas may quite naturally sound a bit like a fancy, but actually, the state of primordial Enlightenment is really present. The whole magic results from recognizing it or not: Enlightenment is gained through recognizing its primordial nature and there is no Enlightenment as long as we have not recognized it. Being Enlightened is merely depending on this simple point...isn't it magical? Though Awakening has always been here, if we do not wake up to Awakening, how is Awakening going to happen?

Sakyamuni Buddha awakened to this absolute reality. He saw how the different primordial wisdoms and bodies or kayas are spontaneously present. He saw that everything is part of this reality and that we are also part of it even though we do not recognize it. There is no difference between the nature of a Buddha, namely a fully awakened being and the nature of an ordinary being or someone plunged in the deepest confusion. From the absolute point of view, there is no difference. The difference merely lies in the fact that Buddha has perfectly recognized Enlightenment, whereas we have not done it yet. This is what makes the difference, not a great deal indeed, isn't it?

At the beginning there is a base, then two paths and hence two fruits

In « The path of Great Perfection» by Patrul Rinpoche who handles the preliminaries of Longtchen Nyingtik, it is told that one day someone arrived in Lhassa to pay a tribute to a statue representing the prince Siddhartha at the age of nineteen. He prostrated at the feet of the statue and then addressed it as follows: « When I think that at the beginning we were both exactly at the same level »! Indeed, at the beginning there is a base...

« But unlike me, you have put all your energy in practising and you have achieved full Enlightenment, whereas my being so lazy has led me to wander again and again in Samsara. I am paying a tribute to you. I am prostrating in front of you. » ...and afterwards there are two ways...and hence two fruits...

Three great types of practices within Dzogchen

1. At the outer level, Semde, the different classes of consciousness.

2. At the inner level, Longde, the different classes of space.

3. At the secret level, Men Ngak, the different classes of essential instructions.

1. At the outer level, Semde, the different classes of consciousness.

Here are a few explanations about Semde. All possible manifested and living phenomena can not be parted nor divided from the mind. It is completely the opposite of our usual perception of the present world, whereby we believe that an objective reality — a reality of a subject/object — does exist. Here, as opposed to this point of view, it is claimed that all possible phenomena are fully part of the mind.

Once Rigpa has been recognized

All possible phenomena are part of the mind. This is the ground point. Being part of the mind does not mean anything by itself. But how is it possible to experience it? It is about Dzogchen here. Rigpa has already been introduced and the nature of mind recognized. Once the practitioner has reached out this stage, he/she has a deep sense that everything is merely the result of interactions within the mind. Claiming that all phenomena are part of the mind is not very lively. But stating that everything seems like our mind interplaying, like a magical manifestation of our mind, sounds much more appealing. Hence we feel it is possible to experience it. Within Dzogchen, the base and the manifestation of the base are always here.

What is the mind like?

The introduction to Rigpa allows to recognize the uncreated dimension of the mind that is beyond any notion of the three times. This is the door of entrance. By then, it is possible to gradually understand how self-existing this wisdom is. Our mind is fundamentally this self-existing wisdom. All other aspects will result automatically in a progressive way. We can gradually be aware that this primordial consciousness has not been fabricated. It is not made of the usual concepts, nor by any notion of "I", nor less by any notion of "before", "after" and "now", related to the three times. As long as we are in this time-related notion, it is obviously not possible to get in touch with this dimension of the space wisdom.

An interplaying magical mind

Then, it will be possible to utter with precision: « As a matter of fact, mind is rather of uncreated or non-fabricated or luminous nature... » For, we would have experienced it within our practice. This is what is called Semde, the different classes of consciousness. It deals with all possible phenomena experienced as the interaction or the manifestation or the magic of the mind. It looks like a reflection of the sun on water, like all possible reflections of the mind, all its glances...

Within Semde, the extreme concept of something that should be abandoned is left aside, whereas it is still present in the previous vehicles. Here, we go far beyond the very concept of abandoning veils or defilements or the lack of recognition. These concepts result from an extreme viewpoint.

2. At the inner level, Longde, the different classes of space. Within Longde, the types of space, we go far beyond the extreme concept according to which there would be some remedy. When we come to the classes of space, everything that may be perceived — for, though it is empty of any "I", there is still "a space of awareness" — is merely experienced as being a mere self-manifested ornament. It sounds rather subtle. Within Semde, the experience consists of perceiving phenomena as an interplaying of the mind. Within Longde, the experience consists of perceiving the different mental and sensitive perceptions as a mere self-manifested ornament.

Turning consciousness into an object

Within Semde, it deals with the manifestation or the unfolding of the mind. There is a very strong notion of a reality called consciousness that is self-existing wisdom. It seems as if consciousness was turned into an object.

Like clouds appearing in the sky

Within Longde — as it aims here at experiencing this special dimension called space — we go far beyond any concept of consciousness. Usually it is said that the nature of mind is either this or that, and we set our consciousness in the middle, even if it is declared that consciousness is "all pervading". But once we have reached out Longde, we are far beyond this kind of representation of a consciousness becoming an object of reality. Every single perceived thing is a mere self-manifesting ornament, like clouds appearing in the sky. We can not say that clouds are produced by the sky.

Within Semde, there is an idea of a womb that is somehow the mind that produces these "offsprings" that are all manifestations. Within Longde, these phenomena are nevertheless like clouds in the sky, like mere self-manifested ornaments. Though there is actually something that is perceived by our senses or by the mental, there is no womb from which something could arise, but instead it merely appears as an ornament. Within Longde we attain a dimension that is even subtler than the notion of consciousness. There we get to something that is highly related to the absolute. At this stage the absolute can no longer be defined as consciousness.

3. At the secret level, Men Ngak , the different classes of essential instructions

Within Men Ngak dealing with the classes of instructions, we go far beyond the "extremes of things to be abandoned or of remedies to be applied". In the first case, we give up any idea of something to be abandoned, in the second case, we go far beyond the idea of any remedy to be applied, and at last in the third case we go far beyond both of them. Practice entails four levels...here we reach out the very point, whereby the more fascinating it becomes, the less we can tell since there are some specific practices that must be done previously ! Moreover there are many commitments to uphold.

3. Ethic (Tib. Tsültrim)

There is one ethic with upholding and another one without upholding.

a) Ethic with upholding

It is about samayas related to flawless body, speech and awakened consciousness. Each of these three samayas entails nine aspects: three upholdings at each of the following levels: the outer, inner and secret ones.

We can not list the twenty-seven samayas. Here are only those related to the flawless body.

Outer samayas

- no stealing;
- No killing;
- no sexual misconduct for married lay people.

Inner samayas

- no criticising one's mother and father;
- no showing disrespect towards one's vajra brothers and sisters;
- no being careless with one's body.

Secret samayas

- no bringing discredit upon dharma;
- no discrediting sentient beings;
- no harming one's body.

b) Ethic without upholding

Ethic without upholding deals with being at the very heart of this self-discriminating wisdom, where there is no longer any notion of good or bad, nor any thing to cultivate, to abandon, to wish or to fear. What is experienced is a state of equanimity, of great completion. Everything is part of this state of unique essence that is uncreated, luminous and loving.

4. Meditation (Tib. Gompa)

Semde, the different classes of mind.

The purpose is here to meditate upon what is called union of emptiness/awareness.

Before that stage, it dealt with the union of emptiness/ manifestation or else called emptiness/bliss. Now we have reached out to the indivisibility of the uncreated absolute, namely Rigpa. We can meditate this inseparable twofold aspect as being Dharmakaya. This uncreated dimension that is pure awareness is the Dharmakaya.

Longde, the different classes of space.

The purpose is to merely meditate the Dharmata, the absolute reality, contemplating it without any single effort.

Men Ngak, the different classes of essential instructions.

The purpose is to meditate on the primordial liberation. We can find out that, as nothing has ever been distorted, so nothing requires to be liberated. Everything is in a liberated state thanks to this luminous uncreated essence. Therefore we aim towards meditating on this primordial liberation "without any notion of something to be abandoned".

And right now, doing it the american way... I am going to introduce you to the nature of mind... no, no I am joking...

Trekchö and Thogal

The "classes of instructions" entail two main instructions: Trekchö, of primordial purity and Thogal of spontaneous presence. Though both practices are inseparable, Trekchö is meant for so-called «lazy» practitioners. They are not said lazy, as it is usually meant, but because there are not able to develop great efforts, unlike practitioners of Thogal. Thogal requires indeed a certain kind of energy. There are special postures. One among the three postures has to be chosen. There are three looks: upwards, downwards or straight ahead. We have to choose one of these three looks. The three postures and the three looks are called the six key points. To allow visions of wisdom to appear during the practice of Thogal, it is necessary to be persevering, persistent and tenacious. Within Trekchö, the purpose is to maintain the degree of awareness in all situations. The practitioner is able, without working through postures, to never losing the view, which is a rather confortable practice. Within Thogal, the practitioner must do some postures that are slightly demanding. Therefore it is said that the Trekchö path is intended for lazy people who are unable to strive themselves that much, whereas the Thogal path, which is related to the spontaneous presence of wisdom lights and Buddha forms, is meant for those who can unfold a lot of energy.

5. Conduct (Tib. Chödpa)

At the outer, inner and secret levels, everything is experienced as an interplaying of the absolute reality. Everything is right and proper since the practitioner stands at the balance point.

It may sometimes happen that some Dzogchen masters show odd behaviour like Do Khyentse Yeshe for example. Some can even be considered as crazy. This is called spontaneous behaviour as the individual is at the very heart of this wisdom, where he can constantly perceive the absolute reality and the illusion of all phenomena, the ornaments that are all phenomena, like a mere play of the absolute.

Like Djamyang Tcheukyi Lodreu who started dancing... Nothing is planned. Even if it may be judged from outside by ordinary people as being weird and showing crazy attitudes, actually every thing is ok.

6. Result (Tib. Drebu)

The result is simple and deep. What is primordially spontaneously present eventually appears.

Conclusion

Talking about the nine yana is an immense topic that has been presented here in a very simplified way while showing its quintessence so as to allow everyone to taste a little bit of it.

Listening, thinking and meditating

One ought to care that the three major principles with respect to listening, thinking and meditating have to always be united. First we listen to teachings, then we think them over and at last we meditate upon them.

Maitreya, the future Buddha declares: « Be aware that if your practice is only based on listening, every single effort is doomed to failure. Be aware that if your practice is only based on thinking teachings over, every single effort is doomed to failure. Be aware that if your practice is only based on meditating, every single effort is doomed to failure».

It is of great matter to learn not to restrict ourselves to only one aspect of the practice. It looks like breathing. Once we have listened to teachings, we think them out by ourselves, deeply, and afterwards we can meditate upon them. Then we start it all over again. This is really a way of life.

Integrating the three great vehicles within ourselves

It is essential to integrate within ourselves the three great vehicles in respect to Shravakas, Bodhisattvas and Vidyadharas.

The groundwork still consists of not being parted away from the experience of renouncement.

Then, we ought to constantly keep the fire of our love and compassion towards all beings strongly alive, which is the main point within Bodhicitta. This wholehearted generosity must always be fostered and developed.

At last, pure vision should enable us to realize that all possible manifested and living phenomena are part of the great purity and great equanimity. This is the foundation of Vajrayana.

When we carefully mind integrating within ourselves these three great aspects, then the path becomes complete.

The entire path

Hinayana

Without renouncement, there can not be any kind of aspiration to free ourselves from suffering and to bring a full stop to it. If we do not have this sense of disgust or weariness, it is just like drinking salted water, our thirst will never stop and so we long for more and more.

Mahayana

If we do not mind cultivating Bodhicitta, namely a great generosity, then, we have not established the foundations of Mahayana, in general and specifically of Vajrayana.

Vajrayana

If we are not able to stand at the heart of this limitless purity regarding all manifested and living phenomena, it would be as if the innermost essence of Vajrayana, namely its vital principle were denied or not even existing.

It is critical to train us understand — not on an intellectual level, but rather through experiencing — first of all the non-self of persons. From that experience, we can enlarge our understanding to the non-self of phenomena. Once we have reached out this stage, quite naturally, it is then possible to get close to the great equanimity within purity.

Regarding the three outer and the three inner Tantras, it is essential, for it is the very essence of samayas, to constantly be moved by trust/ faith and devotion. It has nothing to do with any kind of believes, but instead it means feeling in accordance with. Our whole being is in accordance with this dimension. We have somehow a kind of intuition about it; we can feel it so as to become more and more one with it. Misgivings and doubts have totally disappeared. This is the main point.

Within Dzogchen, no room for misgivings

Trust/faith may be a kind of blind one; in Tibetan, it is said to be « the faith of a fool ». As opposed it may be a certainty that is springing off from scholarship, from practising. In any case, within Dzogchen, there is no doubt for misgivings.

The 5th Dzogchen Rinpoche and the yakboy

Thupten Tcheukyi Dordje, the 5th Dzogchen Rinpoche, was a great master, who was very famous throughout Tibet and considered as a realized lama. One day, an ordinary man, who was looking after his yaks, saw people leaving to the Kham region, where Dzogchen Rinpoche was giving some teachings. As this wise man was called Dzogchen Rinpoche, and he was said to be Dzogchen himself, this yakboy thought that Dzogchen Rinpoche was a scripture. Therefore he was praying for himself to be once able to go and see Dzogchen Rinpoche and the scripture. One day his wish was fulfilled and he started his journey. Dzogchen Rinpoche saw him coming from far away and noticed him. He asked him: « What do you want? ». The man answered: « I want the Dzogchen ». Obviously the yak boy was referring to the scripture. Knowing what it was all about; Dzogchen Rinpoche said to himself that he'd better find an accurate means to bring this man onto the path. So Dzogchen Rinpoche replied: « Ok, I am going to teach you Dzogchen, but first of all, I will give you some instructions you will have to follow. You are going to practise shine, calm abiding, and then you will come back to see me, in three years ». Then this ordinary man went away and practised during three years. He carefully applied each of the instructions given by the lama and three years later he went back to ask Dzogchen Rinpoche again: « Well, now, give me the Dzogchen ». Dzogchen Rinpoche asked him a few questions and he noticed that he had gained a high level of shine.

Blind faith

By then, Dzogchen Rinpoche said to him: « Ok, but you will first practise during three years according to some other instructions I will give you and then you'll come back and see me ». And Dzogchen Rinpoche gave him direct teachings on Dzogchen without telling him that it precisely was the Dzogchen. So, the yak-keeper went back home and three years later once he had recognized the nature of his mind he came back to see Dzogchen Rinpoche. But he did not know about it. So he said to Dzogchen Rinpoche : « Please, now, give me the Dzogchen! ». Dzogchen Rinpoche replied then: «The Dzogchen? This is exactly what you have experienced.» So the yakboy went back to his yaks. Years later, when he was about dying, he realized the rainbow body. This is what is called realization through blind faith.

The awakened awareness of scholars

As opposed, the king Indrabhuti is a good example of the awakened awareness of scholars. When Guru Rinpoche conferred him the fourth empowerment, the king Indrabhuti, thanks to his extraordinary intelligence and exceptional awareness, gained realization and hence liberation.

Once we have come through the door of Vajrayana, it is absolutely necessary to keep trust and faith as well as pure vision alive. This is crucial.

The precious human life

In our present lifetime, we have gained a precious human life, which is difficult to get. As a human being we are endowed with all necessary qualities to access a spiritual path and liberate ourselves. Quite obviously, our human condition can not be reduced to only eating good food and wearing nice clothes. Meaning has to be given to our life and it occurs when we go through this path of knowledge and awareness, at least the path of opening up our hearts. Days go by very swiftly; therefore our life has to be given some meaning. Each second that is elapsing brings us closer and closer to our own death. Being aware of the transient nature of life, and considering that everything that was born is doomed to die, we do strive very hard within our present lifetime and perhaps when dying to get to full Enlightenment. At least, we try our best to be strongly determined to do our utmost within the present given conditions. We keep great hope that through the power of our wishes, we could in our future lifetimes, continue what we have already started in our present life, meet again a master who will introduce us to all these different paths and particularly to Vajrayana, still keeping the strong motivation in mind and longing to help others.

A good dharma practitioner...

Properly practising dharma, while being genuinely rooted in a spiritual path, with pure heart and honesty, will necessarily transform ourselves from within. Everything is becoming easier and lighter in our life. It is just like a great sunshine spreading about in our life. Practising gives the capacity to lighten up the burden of our life. The mind has become clear and peaceful even if we have not totally fulfilled our wish or achieved our goal, at least we have given a sense to our life. We are not seized neither by regret nor fear. Dying will become easy and natural. There is nothing tragic about death. We can understand its whole meaning.

Not giving rise to any kind of pride, but instead remaining modest is also very essential. We should always keep our goal present in our mind. As long as we have not reached it, we ought not to satisfy ourselves with small victories. This is then a good way to help us being humble since we can really estimate what still lies ahead of us, what has to be accomplished. However, if we feel pride, it surely means that a quality is somehow present. We may claim : "I am rich", "I am handsome", "I am beautiful", "My practice is good". Once a kind of bumptiousness has appeared and taken place, indeed we feel swollen and puffed up with pride. But this is totally improper and out of place. These are general instructions that must be explained and repeated again and again.

Khenpo Chimed Rinpoche's biography

Khenpo Chimed Tsering Rinpoche belongs to a family with lineages coming from the great scholar (Acharya) Thomi Sambhota, the most learned persons of the court of king Tritsong Deutsen, and the famous yogi Milarepa. Khenpo Chimed Tsering Rinpoche was born in the beautiful valley of Yolmo, a place that remained hidden for long time with its unique culture, tradition and holy sites blessed by the presence of many heavenly beings such as Padmasambhava and Milarepa.Since childhood, Rinpoche not only displayed a great hability of learning and reading texts but also was educated in the ambiance of faith for Buddha Dharma and compassion for all sentient beings.At the age of eight, he began his Buddhist studies and practiced in his native land of Yolmo.Since this young age Khenpo La retreats regularly in holy Yolmo Valley and received innumerable empowerments from His Holiness Penor Rinpoche, Dudjom Rinpoche, Dilgo Khyentse Rinpoche, Taklung Tsetrul Rinpoche, Dungsy Tinly Norbu Rinpoche, Khenpo Jigmed Puntsok Rinpoche, and Nyoshul Khenpo.In 1976 he received his first empowerment of the Northern Spiritual Treasures (Jang Ter) from His Holiness Dudjom Rinpoche. He also practiced and received many transmissions and empowerments of the Drukpa Kagyu lineage from Lama Dechen Dorje, a disciple of Tripon Pema Choegyal, who was one of the main disciples of the great master Drubwang Shakya Shree.In 1983 Khenpo La joined Dazang Rinpoche's monastery in Kathmandu where he studied the Karma Kagyu lineage. In 1985 he went to South India where he started his further studies on Buddhist philosophical text and practices at Ngagyur Nyingma Institute of Higher Buddhist Studies founded by His Holiness Penor Rinpoche in Bylakuppe. This Institute (shedra) is the largest of its kind in the world. During his studies Khenpo Rinpoche was one of the best students. He also became known for his debate's skill and his capacity for explaining Buddhist philosophy. While he was still a student, he acted as assistant professor in the Institute for five years, and after graduation he became a professor in the same university.In 1996, at the request of many lamas from Yolmo, H.H. Penor Rinpoche sent Khenpo La to teach in different monasteries of his native place. In addition, His Holiness directed Khenchen Pema Sherab Rinpoche and Khenpo Chimed's brother Khenpo Nyima Dondrub to visit Yolmo once a year to teach. In 1999 His Holiness Penor Rinpoche entroned Khenpo La on monastic seat and honored him with Khenpo's certificate (certificate of doctorate). Thereafter His Holiness Pema Norbu Rinpoche rendered permission to Khenpo La to travel all over the world with the teachings of love, compassion and peace given by our great Lord Buddha some 2555 years ago, thus augmenting the ventures auspiciousness. Khenpo Rinpoche visited many European, American, South American, and Asian countries to teach the Buddha Dharma for the welfare of all sentient beings.In 2004 Khenpo La established an NGO and non profitable association named *Siddhartha Foundation* Palyul Dongag Shedrup Wosel Norbu Ling. This project includes the construction of an orphan school, a school for the girls and a retreat center. In the same year, Khenpo Rinpoche started his orphan school named Siddhartha School at temporary school building with 30 orphan children from Himalayan region. The children's number raised with new enrolments every year. At present 100 orphan childrens are having proper education and accomodations in Siddhartha School.Since then, Rinpoche visited various Western & Asian countries to deliver Buddha Dharma's teachings every year for the welfare of all the sentient beings and for the welfare of the orphan children of the Himalayan regions which is the most challenging and ultimate aim of Khenpo Rinpoche.In 2010 Khenpo La started the Siddhartha Foundation project's construction, is happy to take care of his 150 Dharma sons at his school and more than delighted to guide hundreds of disciples all over the world.

Khenpo Chimed Rinpoche's long life prayer

OM SOTTIGYAL KUN NGO WO CHI MED THOD TENG TSALBAR CHED KUN SEL BENZA KI LA YATRIN LEY KUN DRUB KHA DROEE TSOG CHE KHEYDENG DER MON PA DRUB PE GE LEG TSOLNAM DAG DOM SUM TRIM KYI TSA WA TENSEN SAM GOM PE YAL DAB CHE CHER GEYCHED TSOED TSOM PE DRE ZANG YUR ZA WECHI MED YONG DUEE WANG PO TEN SHUG SOLTSA SUM GYAL WA TSOEE JEN LAB DANGCHO NYI NAM DAG CHO CHEN LU MEY THOEDAG CHAG LHAG SAM DAG PAY MON PE DREYGEG MAY LHUN DRUP TRA SHI PAL BAR SHOG

Glossary

ABHISAMAYALANKARA: one of the five treatises of Maitreya written by Asanga.

ARHAT: (Tib. Dratchompa) "Foe destroyer". A shravaka or pratyekabuddha who has attained liberation from Samsara.

BARDO: (Tib.bar do) Intermediate state. Generally refers to the state following death and before the next birth.

BHUMIS: (Tib. Sa) The ten levels traversed by Bodhisattvas. Attainment of the first bhumi means one's first full realization of emptiness. As one progresses through the bhumis, one's realization becomes increasingly deep.

BODHI : (Tib. Djangtchoub) is both a pali and a sanskrit word translated as «enlightenment» but more accurately translated as «awakening» or «to know». The word «Buddha» means «one who has awakened».

BODHICITTA: (Tib. Djangtchoub Sem) it means the intention to attain complete buddhahood in order to benefit all beings. It is classified as ultimate and relative bodhicitta; the latter being divided into aspiration and application bodhichitta.

BODHISATTVA: (Tib. Djangtchoub Sem Pa) is an «awakened courageous one», a Mahayana practitioner who has vowed to attain complete awakening in order to liberate all beings from Samsara. The expression refers to either an ordinary exerting bodhicitta or someone who has attained the realization of any of the ten bodhisattva bhumis.

BRAHMA: is the hindu god of creation and one of the Trimurti, the others being Vishnu and Shiva.

CANDRAKIRTI: (600-c.-650), was a khenpo of Nalanda Mahavihara, the main disciple of Nagarjuna and commentator of his works.

CHAKRAS : (Tib. Khorlo) are wheels of subtle energy located all along the central channel. According to the Buddhist tradition the main chakras are the crown chakra, the throat chakra, the heart chakra, the navel chakra, the sacral chakra and the root chakra.

DAKMEMA : the wife of Marpa. Marpa was translator and root lama of Milarepa. (Also see Marpa).

DHARMADHATU: (Tib. Tcheu Ying) litt. "space of phenomena". The ultimate, primordial expanse of the phenomena of Samsara and Nirvana, which is unconditioned and unchanging. It is emptiness, the absolute reality, not the relative reality seen through a contaminated karma.

DHARMAKAYA : (Tib. Tcheu kyi Kou) "body of truth" the realization of the essence of vipashyana or the result of perfecting the nature of non-conceptuality. In regard to the nature of mind, dharmakaya is mind's empty essence, beyond all speech, thought, and expression. It is also said that it is the non-arising of the mind itself, free from all conceptual elaborations.

DHARMAPALA: (Tib. Tcheu Kyong) Dharma's protector of the teachings. Each of the Tibetan school of Buddhism has its own protectors. The protectors are classified in two categories: the first category comprises the wordly and supra-worldly protectors, and the second category comprises the protectors of wisdom.

DHARMATA: (Tib. Tcheunyi) the ultimate nature or reality of mind and phenomena. Emptiness.

DZOGCHEN (Skt. Maha-ati): "The Great Perfection", the central teaching of the Nyingma school of Tibetan Buddhism regarded as the highest meditation practice and approach to Enlightenment.

KARMIC IMPRINTS: (Skt. Vasana; Tib. Bag-tchag). Habitual tendencies resulting from past lives perceptions which are taught to become «imprinted» in the consciousness.

GORAMPA SEUNAM SENGUE: high master of the Sakya school born in Eastern Tibet in 1429. He founded his own monastery, Tanak Serling, in Tsang area where he taught philosophy. His comments on Madhyamika are among the most important but conflict with the thesis of Tsongkhapa, the founder of the Gelugpa's school.

GOUROU RINPOCHE: Padmasambhava or Padmakara, the Lotus-born, the indian master of tantric Buddhism, born in the 8th century, who through various styles of conventional and unconventional conducts, was primarily responsible for transplanting the teachings of Vajrayana Buddhism to Tibet. Also called The Second Buddha.

GUHYAGARBHATANTRA: root Tantra of the 18 Tantras of the Mahayoga, and the primary tantric text studied in the Nyingma tradition as a key to understand empowerment, samaya, mantras, mandalas, and other vajrayana topics.

HINAYANA: (Tib. Thekpa Menpa) "Lesser Vehicle". It includes the first two yana, the Shravakayana and Pratyekabuddhayana whose result is the individual liberation.

IMPERMANENCE: (Tib. Mitakpa) An impermanent phenomenon means that it arises, abides, and ceases. Gross impermance refers to the changes that can be directly observed with the passage of time by undeveloped minds. Subtle impermanence refers to momentary changes, which generally cannot be directly observed.

INDRA: is the king of the gods or devas. Indra lives on the Meru mount.

INDRABHUTI: One of the kings of Oddiyana, mentioned in the Ka'-thang, the hagiography of Padmasambhava, considering the king as the adoptive father of Padmasambhava.

KADAMPA: «Those who are practising the Buddha's teachings and his advices». Tradition founded in Tibet by Atisha in 1042.

KARMA: (Tib. Le) The principle of cause and effect, the actions and their effects but often used to mean the result of past actions.

KLESHA: (Tib. Nyeun Mong) The negative, deluded states of mind that afflict sentient beings, also known as disturbing emotions. The five root afflictions are ignorance, desire, anger, pride, and jealousy.

LIBERATION: (Tib. Tarpa or Dreul oua) two different meanings are given to the english word «liberation». "Tarpa" refers primarily to the state of freedom from suffering attained in the Shravaka and Pratyekabuddha yana, as opposed to the full awakening of a Buddha attained through the Mahayana. Dreul oua has a vaster connotation, and often refers to the spontaneously available, innate liberation that one connects with through the practices of Mahamudra and Dzogchen, such as in the term «self-liberation».

LOUIS DE LA VALLÉE- POUSSIN : born in 1869 in Liège, Belgium and dead in 1938 in Brussel, is a belgian orientalist. He studied and translated Tibetan.

MADHYAMAKA : (Tib. Umapa) «The Middle Way». The Mahayana school of Buddhism founded by the master Nagarjuna that propounds the absence of true existence of all phenomena. Since the Madhyamaka teaches the union of the relative and ultimate truths in a way that is beyond the two extremes of permanence and nihilism, they are called the «Proponents of the Middle». It is called «middle» because it is beyond the two extremes that are nihilism and eternalism.

MAHAMUDRA: (Tib. Tchagya Tchenpo) «The Great Seal» that seals the vacuity of all phenomena. A tradition of meditation's profound methods based on direct realization of the mind's true nature. The highest of the teachings of the Kagyu school.

MAHAPANDITA RONGZOM: great tibetan master who lived during the 11th century and who was of a leading importance in the renewal of the Nyingma school.

MAHAYANA: (Tib. Thekpa Tchenpo) «Great vehicle». Also called the Bodhisattvayana, characterized by emphasis on both compassion that longs for the liberation of all beings, and on wisdom that perceives the true nature of phenomena. Through entering into this vehicle and progressing along this path, one brings all sentient beings to the state of complete Enlightenment.

MAITREYA: (Tib. Djampa) The Bodhisattva who is now residing in Tushita Heaven. He will be the fifth Buddha this aeon.

MANDALA: (Tib. Kyil Khor) The Tibetan term for mandala literally means «the center and its surroundings». In Vajrayana Buddhism, a mandala is the abode of the yidam or meditation deity, the environment composed of pure appearances of Buddha lands that communicate the essence of the wisdom of Enlightenment.

MANTRAYANA: See Vajrayana.

MARPA: Root lama of Milarepa, and translator. One of the founders of the Kagyu school. His life story is well known through all Tibet due to Milarepa, his foremost disciple.

MATCHIK LABDREUN: (1055-1149) was a renowned Tibetan Tantric Buddhist practitioner and teacher. She was a great Tibetan yogini who originated several Tibetan lineages of the Indian Tantric practice of Tchöd.

MEUNLAM TCHENMO: also known as The Great Prayer Festival. It falls on the 4th-11th day of the 1st Tibetan Lunar month. This is the greatest religious festival in Tibet and was established in 1409 by the great Tibetan philosopher, monastic teacher, and social reformer, Tsong Khapa Losang Drakpa (1357-1419), the founder of the Gelugpa tradition of the Tibetan Buddhism.

MILAREPA: (1040-1123) One of the foremost disciples of Marpa and guru of Gampopa. *Hundred Thousand songs* is the life-story and teaching of this great and beloved tibetan poet.

MIPAM RINPOCHE : (1846-1912) One of the most important masters of the Nyingma lineage and a leading figure in the Ri-me (non sectarian) movement in Tibet. He was accomplished in a variety of subject. He wrote extensively on sciences, philosophy, engineering, grammar, poetry, medicine. He was a disciple of Patrul Rinpoche. He wrote many commentaries on Buddhist sastra and Tantra.

MOKSHA: is the "liberation" from Samsara and the suffering conditioning the cycle of repeated births and rebirths (reincarnation). Moksha means Nirvana.

NADI, VAYU, BINDU: (Tib. Tsa, Loung, Thigle) the channels (Skt. Nadi), winds (Skt. Vayu) and drops (Skt. Bindu) are elements constituting the pattern of the subtle body. The yogic practices are to bring the lung from the side channels to the central channel in order to realize the Clear Light experience, which is the true nature of the mind.

NAGARJUNA: (Tib. Lundrup) Indian philosopher who lived in the late 2nd century AD. He founded the Madhyamaka school of Mahayana Buddhism. A hundred works are attributed to him. Ngggrjuna's primary contribution to Buddhist philosophy is in the use of the concept of sunyata or "emptiness".

NATURE OF MIND: A term for the intrinsic state or true nature of mind; the uncontrived, natural state, also known as «ordinary mind» or the wisdom of self-arisen awareness. Synonym to «the ways things are». Also translated as «natural state», «abiding nature», or «abiding mode».

NIRMANAKAYA : (Tib. Tulku) «Body of manifestation». The form kaya of a Buddha that can appear to both impure and pure beings. It is the fruition that is achieved for the benefit of other sentient beings. Therefore, this kaya is closely associated with compassion. According to history that is held in common, the most recent nirmanakaya Buddha was Shakyamuni Buddha. However, in the Tibetan tradition, Guru Padmasambhava is also considered a nirmanakaya Buddha.

NYUNG-NE: Practice of the Thousand-arm Chenrezig Tantra whereby genyen vows are taken and fastening is practised.

NIRVANA (Skt. Moksha, Tib. Nya-Ngèn-Le-De-pa) Can either mean the liberation (Tib. Thar pa) from suffering achieved through the Shravakayana or Pratyekabuddhayana, or the state of omniscience, complete awakening, achieved through the Mahayana.

NYINGMAPA: «The school of the ancients», the most ancient of the four schools of the Tibetan Buddhism. The Nyingmapa are the followers of the first teachings of Secret Mantra propagated in Tibet by the great master Padmasambhava in the 8th century.

OMNISCIENCE: (Tib. Namkyen) complete Enlightenment or Buddhahood. Buddha is often called «The Omniscient».

UTPALA: is a blue lotus, a symbol of purity. It rises out of the mud with a pristine bloom. Several traditional deities of Tibet including Tgrg are depicted holding Utpala flowers in hands.

UTTARATANTRA: one of the five treatises of Maitreya written by Asanga.

PADMASAMBHAVA: (See Guru Rinpoche).

PARAMITA: (Tib. Pareul Tu Tchinpa) The six perfections that are practices exerted in application Bodhicitta: generosity, discipline, patience, effort, meditation, transcendental knowledge.

PARINIRVANA: (Tib. Yong-su Nyang-dée) the highest Nirvana that is entered at death in contrast to that attained during life.

PATH: (Tib. Lam) the spiritual journey is considered like a path driving, stage by stage, to enlightenment.

PATRUL RINPOCHE: (1808-1887) was a prominent teacher and author of the Nyingma school of Tibetan Buddhism. His beautiful and well-known commentary on the Longtchen Nyingthik Ngondro, the Kunsang Lama Shelung, («The words of my perfect teacher») is a spiritual treasure of the Nyingma school, the oldest Tibetan Buddhist tradition.

PRAJNA: (Tib. Sherab) Wisdom or transcendental knowledge relating to insight into emptiness. Also the naturally sharp discriminating quality of awareness. While prajna functions in our worldly activities, on the highest level it is the awareness that sees impermanence, selflessness, ego-lessness and emptiness.

PRAJNAPARAMITA: (Tib. Sherab Kyi Pareul Tu Tchinpa) transcendent knowledge. The Heart Sutra, a well-known Mahayana Buddhist Sutra.

PRATIMOKSHA: Individual liberation; vows or teachings concerning personal liberation from cyclic existence.

PRATYEKABUDDHAYANA: the yana of the solitary realizer who attains Nirvana chiefly through contemplation of the twelve links of interdependent origination.

RENOUNCEMENT: (Tib. Nge Djung) A mind that, motivated by a feeling of disgust with ego-clinging, wishes to be completely free from the prison of Samsara.

RIGPA: the non-ordinary mind, different from «sem» the conceptual, ordinary mind.

RUPAKAYA: The Sambhogakaya and the Nirmanakaya, the two formal bodies, apparant reflections of the Dharmakaya, that appear to human beings and answer their questions.

SAMADHI: A state of un-distracted meditative absorption or meditative concentration. The definition of samadhi is «a one-pointed mind concerning objects to be examined».

SAMATHA: (Tib. Shine) Calm abiding. Tranquillity meditation. Its aspects are mindfulness (recollection of the objects of meditation) and alertness (continuity of mindfulness). In samatha, distraction toward objects such as form has been calmed and the mind abides one-pointedly in whichever samadhi one is practicing. Tranquillity meditation. "Sama" means «calm» and "tha" means «abiding», so samatha means «calm abiding».

SAMAYA : (Tib. Damtsik) «Sacred bond». Commitments of the Vajrayana path. Samayas essentially consist of outwardly maintaining harmonious relationship with the vajra master and one's dharma friends and inwardly not straying from the continuity of the practice.

SAMBHOGAKAYA: (Tib. Longtcheu Gyi Ku) «Body of perfect enjoyment». In an outer sense, this kaya refers to the Buddhas's manifestations as they appear in celestial realms giving teachings only to the assembly of noble Bodhisattvas by way of light-bodies, rather than physical ones. The Buddhas belonging to the five Buddhas' families taught in Vajrayana Buddhism are Sambhogakaya Buddhas.

SAMSARA: (Tib. Khor-oua) is the cycle of birth, death and rebirth experienced by sentient beings due to their ignorance and whereby suffering is the predominant experience.

SAMSKARA : (Tib. Du Djé) are the imprints left on the subconscious mind by experience in this or previous life which then influence all of life, one's nature, states of mind, responses and so on.

SANTIDÉVA: was an 8th-century indian buddhist scholar at Nalanda University and an adherent of the Madhyamaka philosophy of Nagarjuna.

SARIRA: (Tib. Ring-sel) a kind of pearls that are found among the cremated ashes or buddhist spiritual masters.

SARMAPA: «New translation schools». In the Tibetan Buddhism, the Sarma includes the three newest of the four main schools comprising: Kagyu, Sakya, Geluk. The Nyingma school is the «old translation school».

SEM: the ordinary mind.

SEVEN-BRANCH PRAYER: A form of prayer which comprises seven parts: prostration, offering, confession, rejoicing, requesting the teachers to turn the Dharma wheel, requesting them not to pass into Nirvana, and merit dedication.

SHERAB: superior knowledge. (See Prajna).

SHASTRA: (Tib. Ten Tcheu): A philosophical treatise. Shastras are commentaries on the words of the buddha by pundits, or learned masters of India and Tibet.

SHRAVAKAYANA: (Tib. Nyénteu kyi Thekpa) The yana of the hearer's yana. Hinayana practitioner of the first set of teachings given by the Buddha. The final objective is to become an arhat.

SHUNYATA: (Tib. Tong-pa-nyi) Emptiness, the true nature or such-ness of all phenomena that is devoid of true, inherent, independent existence and is beyond all levels of conceptual elaboration.

SIDDHI: (Tib. Ngeudroub) Accomplishment. The fruit obtained through the practice of the instructions. Common accomplishments can be simply supernatural powers. But the term accomplishment almost refers to the supreme accomplishment which is Enlightenment.

SUTRA: (Tib. Do) Refers to either the Hinayana and Mahayana teachings given by the Buddha, as opposed to the Tantras of the Vajrayana, or the scriptures of the Sutra Pitaka within the Tripitaka, which are concerned with the training in samadhi.

SUCHNESS: (Skt. Tathata) it is a central concept in Buddhism. The synonym Dharmata is also often used. It expresses appreciation of the true nature of reality at any given moment. As no moment is exactly the same, each one can be savoured for what occurs at that precise time, whether it is thought of as being "good" or "bad".

SEED SYLLABLE : (Skt. Bija, Tib. Sa-beun) seed syllable from which the deity of practice or the yidam appears.

TIBETAN BUDDHIST CANON: all the scriptures of the Buddha's speech, the Kagyur with the Tripitaka (the three baskets), and the Tengyur, the fourth basket, that collects Tantra and Shastra.

THREE BASKETS: (Skt. Tripitaka, Tib. Denö Sum) the whole Buddhist canon comprising the Vinaya, the Sutras and the Abhidharma.

THREE JEWELS: The Buddha, the Dharma and the Sangha are the three refuges against suffering.

TSONGKHAPA: founder of the Gelug school of Tibetan Buddhism. He was born in 1357, in the Tsong Kha region of Amdo, in Eastern Tibet. He wrote an excellent commentary on the Guhyasamajatantra. It is said that Sakyamuni Buddha had prophesied the rebirth of Tsongkhapa as an incarnation of Manjushree.

TUMO: the yogic practice of the completion phase which results in the generation of inner heat according to the teachings of Milarepa.

TWELVE LINKS OF INTERDEPENDENT ORIGINATION: also known as «the 12 nidanas». It is a chain of causality that endlessly produces life in Samsara. The twelve links are ignorance, karmic formation, consciousness, name and form, six senses, contact, feeling, craving, grasping, becoming, rebirth and «old age and death».

VAJRAYANA: (Tib. Dorje Thekpa) Tantric teachings of the Mahayana. The secret mantrayana that uses a variety of methods that take the results of awakening as the path. Also called the Fruition Vehicle.

VAJRA: (Tib. Dorje) Diamond, «king of stones». As an adjective it means indestructible, invincible, firm, adamantine, diamond like. The ultimate vajra is emptiness, the conventional vajra is the ritual implement of material substance.

VIDYADHARA: «One who through profound means holds the deities, mantras, and the wisdom of great bliss».

YANA : (Tib. Thekpa) «That which carries», or «Vehicle». A set of teachings that enable one to journey toward rebirth in the higher realms, liberation from Samsara, or complete Buddhahood. There are different classifications of yana, such as a triple division of Hinayana, Mahayana, and Vajrayana; the triple division of Shravakayana, Pratyekabuddhayana, and Bodhisattvayana; and the nine gradual vehicles of Shravaka, Pratyekabuddha, Bodhisattva, Kriya, Upa, Yoga, Maha Yoga, Anu yoga, and Ati yoga.

YESHE TSOGYAL : she was Padmasambhava's main consort and also one of the King Tritsong Detsen spouses. She realized all accomplishments resulting from the practice of Vajrakilaya and was particularly concerned with protecting as well as spreading Padmasambhava's teachings.

YIDAM: a deity representing Enlightenment, in a male or female, peaceful or wrathful aspect in accordance with one's individual nature. The enlightened aspect of the mind's practitioner. The yidam is the source of accomplishment.

YOGA: (Tib. Nel Djor) A method to make one with the natural state. The 6 yogas of Naropa.

YOGI/YOGINI: (Tib. Nel Djor pa/ma) someone who practices yoga, A spiritual practitioner.